OLD THEATRE DAYS
AND WAYS

THE DAYS BEFORE THE QUEUE

The pit door at Drury Lane in 1784.

Fr.

OLD THEATRE DAYS
AND WAYS

By

W. J. LAWRENCE

Author of
"The Life of Gustavus Vaughan Brooke Tragedian"
"Shakespeare's Workshop" etc.

BENJAMIN BLOM   New York/London

First published 1935
Reissued 1968 by
Benjamin Blom, Inc.
Bronx, N.Y. 10452

Library of Congress Catalog Card Number 68-20236

Printed in the United States of America

PREFACE

FIFTY years of intensive study, solid research, and hard thinking have gone to the making of this book. If it be true that wine to be good must be kept for long in bottle, and, when it is to be drunk, carefully decanted, then what I now proffer to theatre-lovers should be good wine. No doubt to the connoisseur the flavour will be unfamiliar, but I trust that it will be none the less palatable. In what follows there will be no twice-told tale. I have purposely confined myself to an easy discussion of certain new aspects of an old but inexhaustible theme. Bygone retailers of theatrical ana—the Dr Dorans and Dutton Cooks of placid Victorian times, at whose feet I sat entranced in my salad days, and for whose work I still retain esteem—were well content to go with the current adown the main stream of stage history, and never troubled to make any exploration of its tributaries. Mine has been the mission to complete the story by remaining alert while lingering for long in the neglected backwaters. Unfortunately, profuse as have been my contributions to periodical literature on a great variety of theatrical subjects, that fact has been little recognized. Aristides was no more wearied over being characterized as the Just than I am over being classified solely as an Elizabethan scholar. It is true that for many years Shakespeare's stage has had for me its persistent fascinations, but not to the exclusion of other interests. The whole theatre has been my province.

Some portions of this book, not amounting in any instance to an entire chapter, and therefore impossible to specify, have already appeared in print. I take pleasure in acknowledging my indebtedness to the editors of *The New Statesman and Nation*, *The Spectator*, *The Daily Telegraph*, *The Stage*, and *The Birmingham Mail* for their courtesy in allowing me to embody in these studies many details originally given to the world in articles of mine published in their columns. Nothing more remains to be said, except that I have taken care to see that the illustrations are worthy of the name, and really illustrate.

W. J. L.

September 1935

CONTENTS

ILLUSTRATIONS

CHAPTER I

THE CEREMONY OF THE DRUM AND TRUMPET

IN those far-off days when the players were nomads and had no permanent housing they had certain customs which were practically universal, and prominent among these was the ceremony of the drum and trumpet. It was an aggressive method of advertisement at a time when methods of advertisement were few. Hand-written play-bills were generally posted up conspicuously in various parts of the town or village visited, but not everybody could read, and something more arresting and immediate had to be devised in order to obtain public attention. The old strollers believed in making a noise in the world, and their more dignified successors in the sock and buskin have ever since striven to emulate their example. After a crowd had been assembled by drum and trumpet one of the executants acted as crier, and announced where and when the performance was to take place. This custom had to fight vigorously for its existence, for Bumbledom at large set its face against it. And no wonder. It is not surprising to find that the ruling powers in town and country in ruder times had a holy horror of crowds, seeing that the mob in those days had great potentialities for mischief-making, and might at any moment run amuck and loot all the stalls. Hence they were perpetually frowning upon the poor strollers with their drums and trumpets. When Anthoine Sené brought his company to Amiens in 1556 he was given permission to act there for a week, provided that in the matter of advertisement he confined himself to the use of posters and made no resort to drum or trumpet.[1] In the same year one Pierre Lepardonneur arrived with his tiny troupe at Rouen, and, after suffering arrest for performing without permission, was, on humble petition, allowed to act, with the understanding that "neither drum nor any other noisy instrument was to be used by him for the assembling of the people."[2]

Whether the ceremony of the drum and trumpet gained early sway in Paris, and, if so, whether it persisted there after the establishment of the first theatres, are points on which there is no evidence. But it is at any rate certain that the practice continued for long in the French provinces. On this score Scudéry's *La Comédie des comédiens*, a play dealing with strolling life, is illuminative. When it fell from the press in 1635, shortly after its production, it was embellished with a composite engraving showing at once the interior and the exterior of a temporary rural playing-place. The upper section of this depicts a stage on trestles, not the sort of arrangement likely to be found in a regular playhouse. Below we see the façade of the building, with a *portier*, armed with a formidable two-handed sword, guarding the entrance. On his left stands a gallantly arrayed drummer a-drumming, and beside him a masked player with sword and buckler. On the walls are hand-written playbills in frames. The absence of the trumpeter is curiously significant. In France and elsewhere from this period the tendency was to dispense with the trumpeter's services, and one might say that henceforth the ceremony was purely one of the drum.

[1] L. Petit de Julleville, *Les Comédiens en France au moyen âge*, p. 345.
[2] *Ibid.*, p. 343.

There is good reason to believe that the custom was established in England about the middle of the sixteenth century, at least a score of years before the first London theatres were erected, and at a time when the players were habituated to performing in the inn-yards. Only one clue to its existence in that period is forthcoming, and the curious thing is that it has not yet been observed. It presents itself in the patent granted to Leicester's players in 1574, two years before the building of Burbage's Theater, the first patent ever given to an English company. It is addressed " To all Justices, Mayors, Sheriffs, Bailiffs, head Constables, under Constables, and all other our officers and mynisters," and authorizes Leicester's Men

> to vse, exercise and occupy the arte and facultye of playenge Commedies, Tragedies, Enterludes, stage playes, and such other like as they haue alredie vsed and studied, or hereafter shall vse and studie . . . as also to vse and occupie all such instruments as they haue alredie practised, or hereafter shall practise, for and during our pleasure. And the said Commedies, Tragedies, Enterludes, and stage playes, together with their musicke, to shewe, publishe, exercise, and occupie to their best commoditie during all the term aforesaide, aswell within our Citie of London and liberties of the same, as also within the liberties and fredomes of anye oure Cities, townes, Boroughs &c whatsoever as without the same, thoroughe oure Realme of England.

Since it cannot be taken that the specific right given to the company to use and occupy musical instruments referred to their use of incidental music in their performances, seeing that the right to act included that privilege, it can only be assumed, vague as is the phrasing, that the extra concession referred to their practice of parading with drum and trumpet. The very fact that they were

authorized to continue the practice shows that somewhere
—probably in the City of London—objection had already
been made to it.

That this is the true interpretation of the reference to
instruments and music is shown by the recurrence of
similar authorizations in royal and other licences, one of
them unmistakable in its terms. On February 16, 1595,
Lord Dudley issued a warrant to Francis Coffyn and Richard
Bradshaw " to travel in the quality of playing and to use
music in all cities, towns, and corporations," and re-
questing countenance for them.[1] A clearer reference to
what is here intended occurs in the patent granted to
Robert Heton in 1629 for the establishment of the King's
Revels Company at Salisbury Court, wherein they are
authorized to use drums, trumpets, and public bills when
they find occasion to go into the country.[2] (The fact that
public bills are specifically mentioned shows that the
posting of bills, as well as the ceremony of the drum and
trumpet, had been objected to.)

It is in the country, however, that we get the first clear
reference to the practice. In March 1583 Worcester's
Men gave great offence to the Mayor of Leicester by
parading through the town " with their drum and trum-
pytts " before they had been given authority to act.[3] This
seemingly indicates a procession of the entire company,
not of the drummer, trumpeter, and crier alone; and it
may be that in earlier times this was the rule. We find
that in 1582 it was customary for fencers, when about to
play their prizes in a playhouse or elsewhere, to pass
through London streets with their drums, the idea being

[1] J. T. Murray, *English Dramatic Companies*, ii, 42.
[2] *Shakespeare Society Papers*, iv, 99.
[3] Sir Edmund Chambers, *The Elizabethan Stage*, ii, 221–223.

LA
COMEDIE DES COMEDIENS

Les
Comediens
du Roy

J van Locbom fecit

A. PARIS.
1635

FRONTISPIECE TO SCUDÉRY'S "LA COMÉDIE DES
COMÉDIENS," 1635

to entice the public to accompany them;[1] and such may have been the contemporary custom of the players. It may be, indeed, that this practice was the first thing to arouse the hostility of the Common Council towards the players, since the assembling and marching of crowds were calculated to create serious disorder.

Perhaps the players compromised in due course by sending out a drummer and trumpeter alone, and contented themselves by making a simple announcement. Of the hostility of the civic authorities to the practice in either form we have an inkling in Lord Hunsdon's promise on behalf of his players in October 1594 that if they were allowed to act at the Cross Keys Inn they would " nott vse anie Drums or trumpettes att all for the calling of peopell together."[2] It would seem that, so far as London was concerned, the practice shortly after this fell into abeyance. In February 1600 Henslowe records the purchase on behalf of the Admiral's Men of " a drum and two trumpets to go into the country," an investment which would hardly have been needed had the company then been accustomed to sending out a drum and trumpet in the city. Some relics of the old practice, however, lingered for long among showmen. A scene in the second act of Fielding's *The Author's Farce* reveals that in the early eighteenth century it was usual for the puppet-showmen of London to send out a crier and drummer in advertisement of their entertainments, and to make a formal proclamation, ending with " God save the King!"

Though the ceremony of the drum and trumpet gave as great offence to the authorities in the country as to the

[1] J. O. Halliwell-Phillipps, *Outlines of the Life of Shakespeare*, sixth edition, i, 348.
[2] Chambers, *op. cit.*, iv, 310.

authorities in town, it failed there to meet with a like suppression. It proved to be one of those things that the strollers would not willingly let die. When Laurence Fletcher daringly took his company to Edinburgh in 1598 he met with so much opposition from the Calvinists of the capital that he was powerless to perform until he contrived to gain the goodwill of the Scottish King and became armed with a royal mandate. It was then, on November 12, that, much to the horror and indignation of the unco guid, he sent out drums and trumpets to signalize his triumph and advertise his opening.[1]

Years later hostility, otherwise inspired continued to be shown towards the old ceremony;[2] so much so that such of the London players as were accustomed to go now and again into the country took the precaution to arm themselves with supreme authority, so as to render all opposition on that score powerless. An instance of this has already been cited from the King's Revels patent of 1629.

The present is an opportune moment to deal with the silly attempts which have been made to associate a quite unobscure allusion in *All's Well that Ends Well* with the old ceremony of the drum.[3] It will be recalled that in Act IV, Scene 3, of the play the First Soldier inquires,

---

[1] *Register of the Privy Council of Scotland*, vi, 42.

[2] The old civic records of Norwich reveal that on December 29, 1660, an order was made by the City Council that " Thomas Knowles & other p̄sons that came to this city to sett vp a play in the same & did beate their drummers [*sic!*] wth out allowance & have played twice or thrice shall not from henceforth act any playe any more in this city vpon payne of incurringe the vtmost penalty the lawe will inflict." But on showing their licence from Sir Henry Herbert, Master of the Revels, they were subsequently forgiven and allowed to act.

[3] *Notes and Queries*, 11th Series, xi, 30, 76; Alwin Thaler, "On Strolling Players and Provincial Drama after Shakespere," in *Publications of the Modern Language Association of America*, xxxvii (1922), 264.

relative to the cowardly Captain Dumain, "What say you to his expertness in war?" and that Parolles mordaciously replies, "Faith, sir, has led the drum before the English tragedians." We are confidently told that the reference here is "to the actors who marched through the City accompanied by a drum and trumpet to call attention to the play they were about to act," or, alternatively, to the practice of strollers in marching across the country to the sound of the drum. Apart from the fact that assumption of the latter-mentioned practice is purely gratuitous, there is no warrant for either conjecture. Remark that Parolles says that Dumain led the drum before the English "tragedians," not "players." To conceive why he made that distinction is to read the riddle. Let us turn, then, to the First Folio. In the fifth act of *Julius Cæsar* we get the stage direction "*Drum. Enter Brutus, Cassius & their Army*," etc., and in the fifth act of *Macbeth* a direction reading "*Drum and colours. Enter . . . Menteth, Cathnes, Angus, and Soldiers Marching*." Clearly what Parolles meant was that Dumain's sole knowledge of warfare was derived in playing the drum in a stage battle.

To the players the whirligig of time brought strange revenges. The day arrived when gentle and simple in the country, including those dressed out in a little brief authority, welcomed the ceremony of the drum as earnest of the pleasant hours to come. There is even evidence to show that where the ceremony was omitted it was missed. Writing of bygone Birmingham theatricals in *The Dramatic Mirror* in 1808, Gilliland says:

> The first regular theatre was erected about the year 1740 in Moor Street, which gave another spring to the proceedings. In the daytime a drummer paraded the town, who

beat the rounds, delivered the bills, and roared out encomiums on the entertainments of the evening, which, however, had not always the desired effect. We have been informed by an eyewitness of the fact that the celebrated Yates had sustained this office, and when we reflect that both himself and Shuter exercised their talents in a booth in Bartholomew Fair astonishment ceases. The house was afterwards converted into a conventicle; it then became a grocer's warehouse, and ultimately the workshop of Messrs Bellamy and Co.

In 1751 a handsome theatre was built in King Street, and opened in 1752 by a company announcing themselves "His Majesty's Servants," from the Theatres Royal, London. These persons expressed a wish that the townsmen would excuse the ceremony of the drum, alleging as a reason—the dignity of a London company. The novelty had a surprising effect; the performers pleased, and the house was continually crowded.

Tate Wilkinson, writing in his *Memoirs* in 1790, dwells upon his rural experiences of thirty years earlier, and points out that it had long been customary in Norwich

for a drummer and trumpeter in every street to proclaim in an audible voice, having been assisted by his shrill notes, without which ceremony the gods would not submit to descend from their heights into the streets to enquire what play was to be acted, nor ascend into the gallery.

He goes on to say that Herbert, the manager of the Lincolnshire circuit, determined while at Grantham to omit the time-honoured ceremony, "wishing to grow more polite," but was forced willy-nilly to resume his rub-a-dub-dubbing.

The Marquis of Granby sent for the manager of the troupe, and said to him, "Mr Manager, I like a play; I like a player; and shall be glad to serve you; but, my good friend, why are you so suddenly offended at and averse to the noble sound of a drum? I like it," said the Marquis, "and all the inhabitants like it. Put my name in your playbill, provided you drum, but not otherwise. Try the effect on to-morrow night; if then you are so thinly attended as you have lately been, shut up your playhouse at once; but if it succeeds, drum away."

Herbert then took counsel with his players, and it was decided to renew the old ceremony. "To their pleasing astonishment," Wilkinson continues,

their little theatre was brimfull on the sound of the drum and Lord Granby's name; after which night they row-did-dow'd away, had a very successful season, and drank flowing bowls to the health of the noble marquis.

That famous country manager the eccentric Jemmy Whitely elected to wear his rue with a difference. According to Bernard's *Retrospections of the Stage*, it was customary with him in the seventeen-seventies, whenever he visited a place of importance, to deck himself out in his Don Felix suit, which was composed of pink silk and white satin, and plentifully bespangled, plus a high feather and a very long rapier, and, followed by a boy with a bell, proceed to the market-place, where he held forth vigorously regarding the wonderful performances he was about to give in the town.

Honest Roger Kemble, from whose loins sprang the most distinguished of English theatrical families, had likewise his own method of advertisement. What this was has been revealed by Walter Whiter, the Shakespearian commentator, in a reminiscence of his boyhood days in Warwick. In each town that he visited Kemble was in the daily habit of indulging the inhabitants with a sight of his players on parade by way of reminding them of their presence in the place. Whiter tells us that somehow certain features of one of these processions had become "photographically lined on the tablets of his mind." Though many years had passed, he had only to close his eyes to find memory bringing to him a vision of a little girl, afterwards known to fame as Mrs Siddons, marching along in white and spangles with the players, and bearing herself with a quaint air of regality, her train being meanwhile borne by a strikingly handsome boy in black velvet, her brother John, who little dreamed that his coming celebrity was already resting on the knees of the gods.

Relative to these processions, a charming legend has sprung up, one which, like most legends, cannot be traced to its source. There is no slightest hint of it in Campbell's *Life of Mrs Siddons* or in Boaden's. We are told that when she was no more than a tiny tot Sarah Kemble was taught to march stiff and straight at the head of her father's company, with hands upraised and balancing a small drum on her crown, what time a player walking behind her beat a skilful tattoo on the sheepskin. From this fact—if fact it be—there has been made a somewhat doubtful deduction. It has been said that this tutoring,

> like the carrying of those water-pots which is said to give Egyptian women their majesty of gait, taught the four-year-old child a carriage so firm and commanding that when she came to play the part of queen and empress no mock crown was too heavy, no tinsel jewels were too splendid, to diminish the glory of her bearing.[1]

But on this point one may be pardoned, perhaps, for entertaining scepticism.

[1] Naomi Royde-Smith, *The Private Life of Mrs Siddons*, p. 68.

Delivering Play Bills in the Country.

My first Appearance 'pon my honour,
Sir, in Hamlet the Great Prince of Denmark.

DELIVERING PLAYBILLS IN THE COUNTRY
From a coloured print in the Harvard University Theatre Museum.

Old customs die hard, and with theatrical folk the ceremony of the drum died hardest of all. Writing in 1797, the pseudonymous author of the *Memoirs of the Countess of Derby* points out that among strollers the strictest economy is practised. Though their printed bills were few in number, they distributed them to the best advantage—that is, "by beat of Drum, in order that their arrival and intentions may be known to every inhabitant. A Drum, on this account, always makes a part of the Property of a Country Company." Quite so, and it is difficult to say when it ceased to be a necessary concomitant. We are assured by John Coleman, in his *Fifty Years of an Actor's Life*, that old Manley, the Stamford manager, was accustomed in the eighteen-forties to send out a drummer to make announcements.

CHAPTER II

THE PROMPTER

IN ancient days the prompter, like the child-souls in *The Blue Bird*, was waiting to be born, knew instinctively that he already had a mission, but received no call. What with the excessive width of the stage in the Greek and Roman theatres and the nature of their architectural backgrounds, there was no place where he could have ensconced himself and given the word without bawling.[1] As Donaldson points out, his absence threw a greater responsibility upon the actors, seeing that, in the conditions, their memories had to be impeccable. In the Roman theatre any material lapse was visited with serious consequences. There the players were all slaves, and the man who forgot his lines received a whipping after the performance.

Thus it was that the prompter could not be born until the drama was reborn (or shall we say, in Mrs Poyser's phrase, hatched over again, and hatched differently?). He was a product of the Middle Ages: the sacred drama and he may be said to have come into the world together. Our first trace of him occurs in a minutely detailed and highly interesting miniature painted by Jean Fouquet in 1461, which gives an unflinchingly realistic depiction of the staging of the *Martyre de Sainte Apolline*, a mystery probably represented at Tours. In this we are shown a

[1] J. W. Donaldson, *The Theatre of the Greeks*, eighth edition (1875), p. 311, lays emphasis on his absence, and cites authorities.

series of elevated compartments arranged in a semicircle and crowded with players and musicians. Only Hell-mouth is stationed below. The upper platform is connected by steps and ladders with the enclosed area below, on which all the important action in the play took place. There, on the bare ground, we see the King directing the torturing of the saint, and a little on his right stands a conspicuous figure in clerical attire and with an imposing tiara on its head. This is the prompter. In his left hand he bears an open book of the play, and in his right a staff. He is pointing with the staff in the direction of the elevated musicians, who are actively engaged in playing, and the inference is that it was with this staff that he gave the signal to whomsoever had to speak, sing, or play next. Since all the players remained from first to last in sight of the audience, and occupied their own particular compartment when not engaged in the acting, he was enabled to fulfil all his duties, single-handed, and, unlike the prompter of later days, did not require a call-boy.

In medieval days certain usages were common in the representation of the mysteries and miracle plays the whole world over. A monk or priest seems always to have officiated as the prompter, and he was probably the same person as had conducted the rehearsals. In the preserved accounts for " the play of St George," as given at Bassingbourne in 1511, there is a record of the payment of 2s. 8d. to John Hobard, " a brotherhood priest," for " bearing the book "[1]—a curious term, but even in the Elizabethan theatre the prompter was known as " the bookholder." Of the care taken in these early open-air

[1] Chambers, *The Medieval Stage*, ii, 140.

performances we get an insight in the oldest known prompt-book, that prepared for *Le Mystère de la Passion*, when it was represented at Mons in 1501.[1] This yields minute details of the staging of the play, the *modus operandi* of the various effects, the distribution of the parts, etc., etc.

As Fouquet's miniature suggests, apparently no attempt was made in the early outdoor sacred drama to hide the prompter from view. A quaint story told by Richard Carew in his *Survey of Cornwall* in 1602, relative to the Guary miracle plays, which were performed in Cornish in earthen amphitheatres, helps to confirm this impression:

> The country people flock from all sides, many miles off, to hear and see it; for they haue therein devils and devices, to delight as well the eye as the eare; the players conne not their parts without booke, but are prompted by one called the ordinary, who followeth at their back with the book in his hand, and telleth them softly what they must pronounce aloud. Which maner once gaue occasion to a pleasant conceyted gentleman of practising a mery pranke; for he vndertaking (perhaps of set purpose) an acter's roome, was accordingly lessoned (beforehand) by the Ordinary that he must say after him. His turn came. Quoth the Ordinary, "Goe forth, man, and show thyself." The Gentleman steps out upon the stage, and like a bad Clarke in Scripture matters, cleauing more to the letter than the sense, pronounced these words aloud. "Oh" (sayes the fellowe softly in his eare), "you marre the play." And with this his passion, the Actor makes the Audience in like sort acquainted. Herein the prompter falles to flat rayling and cursing in the bitterest terms he could deuise; which the Gentleman with a set gesture and countenance still soberly related, vntill the Ordinary, driuen at last into a madde rage, was faine to giue over all. Which trousse, though it brake off the Enterlude, yet defrauded not the beholders, but dismissed them with a

[1] Gustave Cohen, *Le Livre du régisseur pour "Le Mystère de la Passion," joué à Mons en 1501* (Strasbourg, Faculté des Lettres, 1925).

great deale more sport and laughter than 20 such Guaries could haue affoorded.[1]

Continuous prompting sounds to us very quaint and primitive now, but it was practised much later in some of the Continental theatres. While it is doubtful whether such wholesale reminding was done in the Elizabethan playhouses, there is some reason to believe that the prompter was accustomed to do something more than merely give the word to the player when he was out. Memories were apt to be treacherous when there was a frequent change of bill, and we know that in Shakespeare's day no two consecutive performances were given of any play, new or old. From certain metaphorical uses of the word 'cue' in old plays it seems that the Elizabethan prompter was in the habit of giving the actor his first words when he entered. Exactly where he stood cannot be determined, but from Cotgrave's equation of his name in his French-English dictionary with *souffleur par derrière* it is evident that he stood somewhere in the tiring-house, and was seldom, if ever, in sight. It was only a question of time before he would be, in all countries alike, completely hidden. From the days of Thespis to our own the whole directing-force in dramatic representation has been towards higher and higher illusion, though progress has been made by slow and almost infinitesimal increments; and there came a period when the visible presence of the prompter grew intolerable. The only problem was where to secrete him to best advantage. After much experiment two solutions were stabilized, one of which still obtains in the Continental theatres generally, and the other in

[1] The Cornish term for the playbook was 'ordinale,' a diminutive of the *ordo* of the liturgical drama. Hence the 'Ordinary' was the bookholder. In later Cornish plays the stage-manager was known as the 'conveyour.'

all English-speaking countries. Of the two the latter is certainly the superior method. With us it became so customary to place the prompter at the first entrance on the actors' left hand that that side of the stage came to be known in the eighteenth century as the P. S., or prompt side, and the opposite side as the O. P. So familiar had the terms become by 1812 that one finds them cropping up in " Johnson's Ghost " in *The Rejected Addresses*, which took the town by storm in that year.

In the early French theatre a system of prompting akin to ours was adopted, and held good until Molière's later day. Chappuzeau, writing of the duties of the French prompter in 1674, says:

> It is part of his office to stand with the book at one of the wings while the play is going on, and constantly to keep his eyes on it, so as to help any actor whose memory fails him, which in technical language is called *souffler*. Therefore he must be careful and able to distinguish when the actor stops on purpose, and makes a necessary pause, during which he must not speak to him, as it would disturb instead of relieving him. On those occasions I have heard actors tell the over-officious prompter to be quiet, either because they did not need his help, or on purpose, to show that they could trust their memory, though it might, indeed, sometimes forsake them. He, therefore, who prompts must do it in a voice which, as far as possible, can be heard on the stage without reaching the pit, in order to avoid calling forth the laughter of certain spectators, who laugh at everything, and who burst out into mirth at passages in the play where others would not even smile.[1]

What requires to be particularly noted is that specialization of function set in in the French theatre much earlier than in the English. With us, from Restoration days on,

---

[1] Quoted in the translation of K. Mantzius, *A History of Theatrical Art in Ancient and Modern Times*, iv, 99.

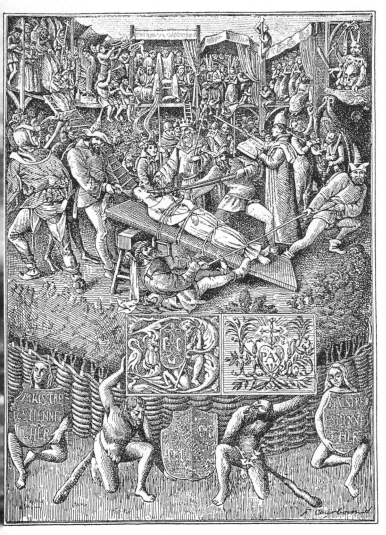

THE MARTYRDOM OF ST APOLLONIA
After Jean Fouquet's miniature.
From Germain Bapst's *Essai sur l'histoire du théâtre.*

26

the prompter has had a multiplicity of duties, but, irrespective of the fact that it was for long his office to copy out the parts, the French prompter has never done anything but prompt. In Molière's day much of the work that then devolved upon the English prompter fell to the lot of the *premier garçon de théâtre* (afterwards known as the *régisseur*), a functionary who had four assistants, two to act as call-boys and two to attend to the properties. The fully marked book which we call the prompt copy was, and is, handled by the *régisseur*, and it is still his business to 'warn' the players.

What for distinction sake is called the Continental system of prompting—in opera it has been practised in many countries—consists in placing the bookholder in a low hooded box centrally at the front of the stage, formerly known in France as the *capot*, and latterly as the *niche à capuchon*. At what time and in which country it originated must remain a matter for speculation. One can only approximate the period of its upspringing. From plans of the house that have been preserved it is certain that when the Théâtre-Français was built in the rue des Fossés-Saint-Germain in 1689 the *capot* was established there. No earlier trace of it can be found, but it would be idle to assume that this was its origin. My own opinion is that, like the orchestra well, the *capot* owed its inception to the Italian opera, and was first seen in Venice about 1635, when the first known public opera-houses were established there. The expanding vogue of the new music-drama would account, as nothing else accounts, for the widespread diffusion of the principle of the visible prompter's box all over the Continent. It may, indeed, have been first brought to France in 1671, when the first French opera-house was erected in the rue des Fossés-de-Nesle.

For aught one knows to the contrary the concealing hood of the prompter's box may have been a later addition, since there is evidence that in one country at a comparatively early period the prompter sat in full view of the audience. The Rev. Mr Clarke relates that when, in his capacity as chaplain to the Earl of Bristol, the English Ambassador, he first visited a Spanish theatre in 1762

> the prompter's head appeared through a little trap-door above the level of the stage, and I first took him for a ghost, or a devil, just ready to ascend to these upper regions; but I was soon undeceived, when he began to read the play loud enough for the actors and the boxes, too, who were near him.[1]

We have here an early indication of the grave disadvantages of the Continental system, for it encouraged indifferent memorization on the part of the players, and led in many places to continuous prompting. Not, of course, that it was without its merits. As Dutton Cook has pointed out, when it is followed the prompter

> cannot possibly be seen by the audience; he can conveniently instruct the performers without requiring them to ' look off' appealingly, or to rush desperately to the wing to be reminded of their parts; while the sloping roof of his temporary abode has the effect of directing his whispers on to the stage, and away from the spectators.[2]

It sounds extraordinary to learn of an eighteenth-century prompter sitting openly to view, but the surprise diminishes when one hears of the same illusion-marring

---

[1] *The Theatrical Review*, May 1763, p. 178.
[2] Dutton Cook, *A Book of the Play*, chapter on " Stage Whispers."

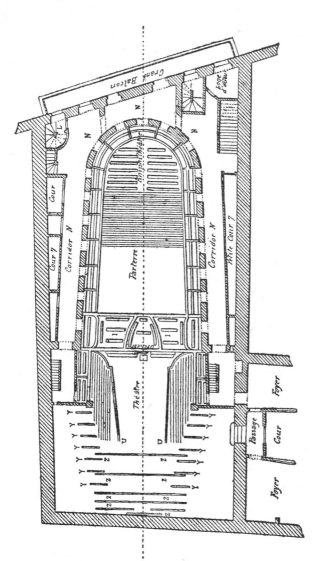

BLONDEL'S GROUND-PLAN OF THE THÉÂTRE-FRANÇAIS, BUILT IN 1689

From K. Mantzius, *A History of Theatrical Art in Ancient and Modern Times*

practice in quite recent times. An English tourist who paid a visit to the Teatro Politeama in Genoa one night in 1890, when the opera of *La Gioconda* was in the bill, was astonished to find that there was no prompter's box, and that the *suggitore* sat in his place without any attempt at concealment, and with his score leaning against the footlights.

But Spain mended her ways, and, having duly hooded the prompter, decided to remain faithful to the *capot*. In the Spanish theatre of to-day the man who gives the word is reckoned quite an important functionary, and his name often appears in the bills. Most of the houses give performances seven days in the week, and twice daily; and, on account of the amount of work entailed, there are generally two prompters to every company. Having a powerful trade union of his own, the Spanish prompter is an individual who, assuredly, is not to be trifled with.

Obviously, though many Spanish theatres have two prompters, they are not expected to work together. Yet elsewhere that has been done. A little more than a score of years ago, when Florencio Parravicini founded a national drama in the Argentine, consisting of light satirical comedy, somewhat primitive conditions for long obtained. Plays were written only a week before their production, and forgotten a week later. Runs were unknown, and revivals rare. In the course of an article dealing interestingly with this strange blossoming Mr Edward Hale Bierstadt writes:

> The short interval between the writing and the production of the play necessitates the use of two prompters, one of whom is stationed in the prompter's box, and the other in the

wings. The last reads the script aloud a few lines ahead of the cast, who pick up their speeches from him as they go along, with amazing facility. Sometimes a cast will never have read the play they are about to perform, and will hardly know whether it is a comedy or a tragedy until after the opening. It would seem that productions given in this fashion would be ragged enough, but it is not so. Long training has given the players such ease in their difficult task that if one did not know the actual conditions beforehand he would never suspect them from the performance itself.[1]

In France, as in Spain, the *capot*, once it had come, had come to stay. Vainly, in 1782, did Patté complain, in his zeal for theatrical reform, that its presence disquieted the players and annoyed the public.[2] Possibly his protest might have proved efficacious had he had any better alternative to offer than the *souffleur's* removal to the orchestra. That was never tried, but something not unlike it was. When Kotzebue, the German dramatist, visited Paris in 1804 he remarked that the Académie de Musique (otherwise the Grand Opéra) had no regulation prompter, and that his duties were fulfilled by the conductor. This apart, there was no deviation from the old routine until December 14, 1899, when Sarah Bernhardt, on opening the old Théâtre des Nations as the Théâtre Sarah Bernhardt with a revival of *Hamlet*, removed the familiar hooded box and made the prompter officiate in the English way. Sarah's innovation, however, proved to be no more than a momentary eddy on the stream: the current ran on as before.

Once upon a time, when, in a musical piece dealing with theatrical life, the *capot* was pressed into dramatic service, an amusing *contretemps* occurred. At Brussels in

---

[1] Article in *The Bellman* for February 1919.
[2] P. Patté, *Essai sur l'architecture théâtrale*, p. 203.

1747 was played an *opéra comique* entitled *La Répétition interrompue*, presenting a scene in which an actor and the prompter quarrelled. In the house was an *officier général*, who happened to be in charge in Maréchal Saxe's absence, and he was stupid enough to make the mistake of taking the quarrel as real. Bristling with indignation over the supposed interruption of the performance, he rushed out of his box, called the guard, and had the two unfortunates arrested.

Others than regulation prompters have sat occasionally in the *capot*, and two of them now bear distinguished names. When the Théâtre Déjazet first opened its doors on September 27, 1859, a new play was produced there called *Les Premières Armes de Figaro*, and its young author, Victorien Sardou, officiated in the *souffleur's* box. Déjazet, who played Figaro, would allow nobody else than Sardou to prompt her, because he alone, in her opinion, was fully acquainted with the various junctures when she was liable to dry up. Since women, as a rule, are quicker studies than men, and have more retentive memories, this particular nervousness on Déjazet's part is somewhat remarkable.[1]

Writing in his engrossing *Souvenirs*, M. Antoine, the noted founder of the Théâtre Libre, tells us how, as a boy, he was taken to the Gaîté by an actress friend to see *La Chatte blanche* and placed in the prompter's box:

A cette époque, la féerie était encore vivante, parée de ses séductions enfantines; toute la soirée, je vis se dérouler les magnificences des trucs et des changements à vue; sous mes yeux, au ras du plancher de la scène, les trappes silencieusement entr'ouvertes me laissant apercevoir les machinistes tirant de petits anneaux accrochés aux talons des artistes

[1] Georges Cain, *Anciens Théâtres de Paris*, p. 139.

pour des métamorphoses stupéfiantes. Cette initiation, par
l'envers du théâtre, ne détruisit pas mes illusions; au con-
traire, elle a probablement éveillé chez moi un goût passionné
de la mise en scène.

Of the abuses to which of old the *capot* led there is
ample testimony. Writing in 1809, Schlegel, in treating
of the Italian players, says:

> They seem to have no idea that their parts can be got by
> heart, and hence, in the Italian theatre, we hear every piece
> as it were twice over, the prompter speaking as loud as
> a good player elsewhere, and the actors, in order to be
> distinguished from him, bawling most insufferably. It is
> exceedingly amusing to see the prompter, when, from the
> general forgetfulness, a scene threatens to fall into confusion,
> labouring away, and stretching out his head like a serpent
> from his hole, hurrying through the dialogue before the
> different speakers. Of all the actors in the world I conceive
> those of Paris to have their parts best by heart; in this, as
> well as in the knowledge of versification, the Germans are
> far inferior to them.[1]

That the German players were in nowise superior to the
Italians in the matter of memorization is shown by what
Kotzebue had written four years earlier:

> Our actors are very content on the boards when they
> come to the end of their *rôles* with the aid of the prompter,
> without which they cannot proceed for long: they know
> nothing by heart. A French actor, on the contrary, never
> misses a word: he speaks as if his part came from his heart,
> and has thus never any need of the prompter. Would that
> it were so in Germany![2]

To what extent, if any, the principle of the *capot* then
prevailed in Germany it would be difficult to say. In

[1] Schlegel, *Dramatic Art and Literature* (London, 1846), p. 228. *Cf.* Joseph
Forsyth, *Remarks on Italy* (1824), i, 68.
[2] August Kotzebue, *Souvenirs de Paris en 1804* (Paris, 1805), ii, 67.

Vienna something like the English system was practised. In the English version of her book on Germany, issued in 1813, Mme de Staël is represented as saying:

> Memory is infinitely more cultivated by the French than by the German actors. The prompter at Vienna used to furnish most of the actors with every word of their parts; and I have seen him following Othello from one side of the scene to another, to prompt him with the verses which he had to pronounce on poniarding Desdemona.

Leaving the question an open one, it remains to be noted that Russia, like France and Spain, has been unswerving in her allegiance to the hooded box. Yet that allegiance has involved the suffering of torture by generations of prompters. Listen to what Constantin Stanislavsky has to say on this score:

> If you look into the kennel of the prompter you are reminded of medieval inquisition. The prompter in the theatre is sentenced to eternal torture that makes one fear for his life. He has a dirty box lined with dusty felt. Half of his body is beneath the stage in the dampness of a cellar, the other half, at the level of the stage, is heated by the hundreds of lamps in the footlights on both sides of him. All the dust created at the rising of the curtain or the sweeping of robes across the stage strikes him square in the mouth. And he is forced to speak without stop during performance and rehearsal in an unnaturally squeezed and often strained voice, so that he may be heard by the actors alone, and not by the spectators. It is a well-known fact that three-quarters of the prompters end with tuberculosis. Everybody knows this, but no one tries to invent a more or less decent prompter's box, notwithstanding the fact that our age is so rich in invention.[1]

A certain grim irony attaches itself to this moan. It lies in the fact that, although Stanislavsky was chief

---

[1] Constantin Stanislavsky, *My Life in Art*, p. 297.

OPENING OF THE THÉÂTRE HISTORIQUE, PARIS, 1847

among the purposeful iconoclasts of the Moscow Art Theatre, and largely instrumental in sweeping away the cobwebby conventions which clogged the Russian stage, yet the vicious old system was allowed to remain. It is not as if there were no alternative: of a surety the English system, in its various forms, was worthy of consideration. It does not suffice to say that there are no longer wings for the prompter to stand in. A hint might have been taken from what Percy Fitzgerald put on record in a pleasant book fifty years ago. While discussing the various methods of prompting he pointed out that many English theatres " have a kind of slight screen that folds back, and which helps to hide the prompter"; also that " at Drury Lane a hole is cut in the pillar, through which the prompter projects his voice." [1] In his eyes the advantage of the English method is that the word is directed straight to the actor's ear, not to his face.

England, having what she deemed a superior method, has never taken kindly to the *capot* in the theatre proper, though circumstances have ordained that it should crop up occasionally in various houses for close on a hundred years. With us it was first seen at the Italian opera-house in the Haymarket early in the eighteenth century, probably during the reign of Queen Anne. (Wherever an Italian opera-house has been set up—no matter how far afield; mayhap in Mexico or Buenos Aires—there the *suggitore* and his hooded box are to be found.) There, most likely, the *capot* and the principle of the encore came into the country together. This, however, is largely inferential, as the earliest reference to the employment of the visible prompter's box at Vanbrugh's old house

[1] *The World behind the Scenes* (1881), p. 211.

occurs in *The Yearly Chronicle for 1761*.[1] While seated at the opera and breathing a different atmosphere John Bull was adaptive enough to shed his insular prejudices, but what he thought about the *capot* on after-reflection is conveyed to us in a humorous episode which formed part of the new prelude to *The Beggar's Opera Reversed*, when Gay's perennial satire was revived under quaint conditions (the male parts being played by women and the female by men) at the little theatre in the Haymarket in 1780. Shortly after the curtain drew up a stage carpenter popped his head up through a trap midway in the boards, and was immediately confronted by the prompter, who came on in a fury to demand what he meant by this irruption. Honest Chip replied that he had opened the trap on his (the prompter's) behalf, having been informed that everything was to be done exactly in the same manner as in the house on the other side, meaning the Italian opera-house. " Psha! " snorted the prompter. " None of your Italian tricks with me! Shut up the trap again! I shall prompt in my old place, for we won't do all they do on the other side of the way till they can do all we do on ours."

This proved fairly prophetic. The Continental style of prompter was unable, from his isolated position, to perform all the duties which fell to the lot of the English prompter in the days before the stage-manager became a power in the theatre. That, too, gives the reason why the *capot* was never adopted to any appreciable extent in our country. It is true that in the nineteenth century it was seen occasionally at the St James's, the Lyceum,

[1] See the extract in Smith's *Compilation for a History of the English Stage*, vol. x (British Museum press mark, 11826 r).

and other theatres during the periods when French players and singers came over here for a season; but its employment in an English theatre for English plays was exceptional. In the book already referred to Percy Fitzgerald states that " during the last days of the old Haymarket the French system was adopted, but it will never be in favour here." As the Haymarket of Fitzgerald's day was built in 1825, one is probably correct in surmising that the period he refers to came pretty early in the century, but in that case his statement admits of no verification. There is a view of the interior of the old Haymarket in Gilliland's *The Dramatic Mirror* (vol. i, p. 151), published in 1808, in which something resembling a *capot* is to be seen at the front of the stage, but, if one, it does not seem to have been placed centrally.

With the introduction of scenery to our stage at the Restoration the prompter had a number of extra duties thrust upon him, which he carried out until the days when the stage-manager arose with a superior authority and took over some of his work. What these were may be readily surmised from a humorous essay by Aaron Hill which appeared in the first number of a bi-weekly journal called *The Prompter*, issued on November 12, 1734, and is proffered in elucidation of its title. To begin with we learn from this that, besides prompting the actor when he was out, it was the business of the prompter to give him the first words of every important speech. This alone kept him pretty busy, but, not to speak of the necessity to warn all the players by means of the call-boy, he had sundry other matters to attend to:

Among his *Instrumenta Regni*, his Implements of Government, I have taken particular notice of a little bell, which hangs over his arm; by the Tinkling of this bell, if a lady in tragedy be in the spleen for the absence of her lover, or a hero in the Dumps for the Loss of a Battle, he can conjure up soft musick to soothe their Distress; nay, if a wedding happens in a Comedy, he can summon up the Fiddlers to dispel care by a Country Dance. . . . Another Tool of his Authority is a Whistle, which hangs about his neck. This is an Instrument of great Use and significance: I won't say but the Sound of a Boatswain's whistle may be sometimes more terrible;[1] but I am sure it cannot be more punctually obeyed. Dr Faustus's celebrated Wand has not a more arbitrary and extensive Power than this Musical Machine; at the least blast of it, I have seen Houses move, as it were, upon Wings, Cities turned into Forests, and dreary Deserts converted into superb Palaces: I have seen an Audience removed in a moment from Britain to Japan, and the frozen Mountains of Zembla resembling the sunny vales of Arabia Felix: I have seen Heaven and Earth pass away, and Chaos ensue, and from thence a new creation arise, fair and blooming as the Poet's fancy; and all by the magic wonder-working whistle.[2]

This explains some of the mysterious marginalia in old Restoration and eighteenth-century prompt-books, wherein R means 'ring' and W 'whistle.' That scenery continued for long to be changed in full sight of the audience at the sound of the whistle is indicated by a passage dealing with "murderous melodramas" at the opening of the seventeenth chapter of *Oliver Twist*.

There are some jobs which even in these days of the rivalry of the sexes still remain the prerogative of mere male man, and the bookholder's job is of them. Yet long before the feminist movement acquired any impetus the woman prompter had emerged. But she was, in very sooth, a solitary phenomenon. Like Mlle de Maupin,

---

[1] Evidently an allusion to the dreaded raids of the press-gang.
[2] For the duties of the later eighteenth-century prompter see John O'Keeffe's *Recollections*, ii, Appendix, p. 422, lines on Wilde, the Covent Garden prompter.

INTERIOR OF NAPOLEON'S THEATRE IN THE TUILERIES

38

Charlotte Charke, that eccentric daughter of Colley Cibber, was one of those unsexed or double-sexed creatures of whom it might be said that they were cut out for men, but the devil ran away with the pattern. In 1752, after she had masqueraded for many years as a man and experienced many vicissitudes, Charlotte adventured upon Bath, and somehow persuaded Simpson of the Orchard Street Theatre to give her the post of prompter. In undertaking the work she resumed her petticoats, but, whether it was that the unwonted garb proved fatiguing after a long freedom of limb, she soon tired of the job, and relinquished it at the end of the season.

There was an intermediate period in the history of the English prompter, lasting almost to within living memory, when he too, like his Continental brother, sat in a box. This took the form of a padded and hooded armed chair, which had the double advantage of throwing out his voice towards the stage and preserving him from draughts. It was in use at Drury Lane as early as November 1775. At that period we find that highly temperamental actress Mrs Abington writing the following undated note to her much-tried manager:

> Mrs Abington has great complaints to make to Mr Garrick respecting a servant in his theatre for very impertinently writing against her in the newspapers last night, only for begging leave to sit in the prompter's box to see one act of a play on a night that she was to perform in *Bon Ton*; when her head was dressed, ready to begin the farce, which was the reason she could not conveniently go to any other part of the house.[1]

That the box was still in regular use half a century later can be gleaned from Edward Fitzball's *Thirty-five*

[1] *The Life of Mrs Abington* (London, 1888), p. 75.

Years of a Dramatic Author's Life, wherein the writer pays genial tribute to the memory of Davy Grove, who was prompter at the Adelphi in 1833, when his melodrama *The Soldier's Widow, or The Deserted Mill,* was produced there:

> Davy had a great horror, not of me, but of what he called my abominable introductions to the perfect upsetting of the regular business of the regular stage. In what he termed the *rational* scenes of the *rational* drama, he could sit quietly in his stuffed chair, P. S. (something like the old Charlies before the new police came in), and give the word, or ring up, or down, without stirring from his seat the whole evening; take a nap at intervals, and all went well. Now, thanks to my monstrous example, there was to run about the stage the whole night; to ring up this trap, to ring down that; signals to be made, with flags, as if one were working a telegraph, and not a theatre. Of such a nature were poor Davy's lamentations over the new-fangled system of ruin, as he termed it, till he retired from the stage, most respected, and, I am happy to add, perfectly independent.

At home and abroad in the old days the prompter was generally a disappointed actor, or some hardy veteran who, on retiring from the stage, had been compelled to take up the work through lack of means. John Downes, the celebrated Restoration prompter, who lives in memory as the author of *Roscius Anglicanus,* a valuable chronicle of his theatrical times, was of the former order. A few other bookholders have emulated his example, notably William Rufus Chetwood, who wrote a quaint and not altogether useless *General History of the Stage,* and Robert Hitchcock, the author of that *Historical View of the Irish Stage* regarding which John Kemble, the tragedian, wrote to his friend Edmund Malone that it was " full of wretched blunders in facts and stuffed with whole pages of follies in opinions."

Richard Brinsley Sheridan once said that " an intelligent prompter is of the greatest importance in a well-regulated theatre. A stage-manager is only required for State days and holidays, but a steady prompter is the corner-stone of the building." It is long now since that held good. With the decline of resident companies, the abandonment of repertory, the vogue of long runs, and the inception of the touring system, the prompter was ousted from his pride of place by the stage-manager, and he in his turn came to play second fiddle to the producer. To-day the prompter is an unconsidered trifle, a negligible quantity: officially he can hardly be said to exist. Work that once demanded a skilled hand can now be done—so far as it is done—by anybody and everybody. Of the dry-rot that set in forty years ago an incident related by Mrs Patrick Campbell in her memoirs is mordantly illustrative. During the first run of *The Second Mrs Tanqueray* at the St James's there came a night when her memory betrayed her, and when she looked for the word the prompter was missing. There was an ugly hitch, and everything was at a standstill until George Alexander went off to procure the book.

CHAPTER III

COMPLEX ADMISSION SYSTEMS

WRITING in 1582 in his *Plays confuted in Five Actions*—only a year or two after the first London theatres were built—that renegade playwright Stephen Gosson revealed a crafty practice of the young bloods of the time. "In the playhouses of London," he says, "it is the fashion of youthes to go first into the yarde, and to carry their eye through every gallery; then, like unto ravens, when they spye carion, thither they flye, and press as near to the fairest as they can." To those unacquainted with the curious characteristics of the Elizabethan theatre, whose knowledge, mayhap, stops short at the fact that the old yard was the rude prototype of the once full-sized pit, it will be a puzzle to determine how this manœuvre was effected. Even astute theatrical antiquaries were mystified about the matter until one of the brotherhood came across the particular passage in the second edition of Lambarde's *Perambulation of Kent* (1592) [1] wherein it is pointed out that those going on a pilgrimage to Boxley were not admitted free any more

> than such as goe to Paris garden, the Bell Savage, or Theater, to beholde Beare-baiting, Enterludes, or Fence play, can amount of any pleasant spectacle, unless they first pay one pennie at the gate, another at the entrie of the Scaffolde, and a thirde for a quiet standing.

[1] The passage is not in the first edition of 1576, but the similitude would probably apply in most respects to that period.

Evidently in those days, at all places of amusement alike, unless the pleasure-seeker was prepared to put up with the roughest of accommodation, there was no means of gaining admission by one single payment to any part of the house. Some light is thrown on the point by Thomas Platter of Basle, who, in the chronicle of his visit to England in the autumn of 1599, gives some account of his experiences at the play:

> Thus, every day at two o'clock in the afternoon in the city of London two and sometimes three comedies are performed, at separate places, wherewith folk make merry together, and whichever does best gets the greatest audience. The places are so built that they play on a raised platform, and every one can well see it all. There are, however, separate galleries, and there one stands more comfortably, and, moreover, can sit, but one pays more for it. Thus, anyone who likes to stand below pays only one English penny: but if he wants to sit they let him pass through a further door, and there he gives another penny. If he desires to sit on a cushion in the most comfortable place of all, where he not only sees everything well, but can also be seen, then he gives another English penny at another door. And in the pauses of the comedy food and drink are carried round amongst the people, and one can thus refresh himself at his own cost.[1]

Inconvenient as this system must have been for the better-class playgoer, it lent itself to what was vital to the player, a swift allocation of the receipts. The players in those days were the virtual tenants of the house, yet they paid no rent—that is to say, for them quarter-day never came. Lessors and lessees alike got rapid returns, and both were paid purely by results. In lieu of a stipulated rent the house-owners (or housekeepers, as they were then called) received a certain portion of the daily receipts, and the players, who were banded together on

[1] Chambers, *The Elizabethan Stage*, ii, 364–365, where the original is also cited.

the sharing system, got the rest. There were not then, as now, separate outer doors of admission to all parts of the house. Even the largest theatres, the Globe and the Fortune, had no more than two entrances—a door for general admission and a tiring-house (or what we should now call a stage) door, through which a few favoured spectators (principally those who occupied stools on the stage) were admitted. But the vast majority of playgoers entered through the theatre door proper, and paid there a preliminary fee of admission, which, however, admitted free to the yard. As Platter indicates, further payments had to be made inside, according to the part of the house visited. Concerning the allocation of receipts, seeing that the Elizabethan era covered a space of sixty years, it is not surprising to find that the system of division varied from time to time and from theatre to theatre. In the early days of Burbage's Theater the players there got no more than the takings at the outer doors, but later on, when they removed to the Globe, they were granted a moiety of the other receipts.

So distinctive were the physical characteristics of the Elizabethan theatre and the method pursued in it of a diurnal division and distribution of the receipts that one is apt to jump to the conclusion that the allied system of a preliminary admission charge with cumulative payment must, of necessity, have been peculiar to our own country. But to reason thus would be to blunder badly. The same system was practised at one time or another in other countries, and in two of them at least—France and Spain—at periods within the Elizabethan era. By what means its seeds were carried (if carried) from country to country, and precisely when they germinated, or whether

INTERIOR OF THE HAYMARKET, 1808

[See p. 37.]

44

in some countries its uprise was due to the architectural defectiveness of the theatres—these are questions which admit of no ready answer.

It is remarkable that French theatrical historians, noted as they are for carefulness in research and acumen in marshalling detail, have not observed that the system of payment by instalments obtained for a considerable time in France, though they themselves have advanced all the facts from which that conclusion can be satisfactorily deduced. To procure the necessary evidence one has only to examine the characteristics of early French theatrical architecture. It was sadly deficient, and in its deficiencies lies the secret. Since the Hôtel de Bourgogne, the first regular French playhouse, dated from 1548, a beginning was made too early to profit by foreign example, and progress was delayed for long by the habit of setting up theatres in already existing buildings, mostly tennis-courts, which, being long and narrow, were ill-adapted to the purpose. What inconveniences playgoers had to suffer are indicated by the fact that no such thing as a circulating corridor was provided in any part of the house until Richelieu built the Palais Royal in 1639. (The Elizabethan theatre, in this respect, was hardly in any better case.) Conforming to type, the earlier theatres had three divisions, a standing pit and two tiers of side balconies, yet there was only one entrance-door. In the angles at the back of the pit were two spiral staircases leading to the balconies. The only means of getting to the seats above was by entering through the pit. Though there were three divisions in the house, there were only two prices of admission. Generally speaking, down to near the middle of the seventeenth century the charges were five sols to the pit and ten sols to the balconies.[1] Since checks had not yet begun to be issued, it is plain to be seen that everybody who entered the theatre had to pay an initial charge of five sols, admitting to the pit, and that those who went upstairs had subsequently to pay another five. It was simply architectural defectiveness which necessitated cumulative payment; here the system served no ulterior purpose; there was never any division of the receipts between two parties, as in England. Speculation is risky, but it may be, viewing the earliness of its establishment, that the architectural characteristics of the Hôtel de Bourgogne and the method of collecting money there were not without their influence on the first Elizabethan theatres and the players who occupied them.[2]

Spain had her initial period of open-air courtyard performances, much akin to the pre-theatrical inn-yard performances in London, and it was not until 1579 that Madrid could boast of a permanent theatre. It was built by Alberto Ganassa, a much-travelled Italian comedian, who was already very popular in Spain, who previously and afterwards visited Paris with his company, and who, very possibly, may have found his way at some time to London. Whether it was introduced by him then or adopted a little later, it is certain that the principle of a preliminary admission charge, giving access to the standing pit, with further demands for the other parts of the house, was established early in the history of the Spanish theatre, and maintained for long.[3] It is noteworthy that when it was abandoned it left behind it a

[1] V. Fournel, *Curiosités théâtrales* (1878), Chapter IX.
[2] For the physical conditions of the early French theatres see Germain Bapst, *Essai sur l'histoire du théâtre*, pp. 369–370.
[3] Glenn Hughes, *The Story of the Theatre* (1928), p. 142.

curious relic. What that was can be best understood, after the prefatory explanation that *entrada* was the by-gone term for the first payment, just as in England it was called 'the entrance,' by grasping the import of a statement in Henry Lyonnet's interesting book dealing with the Spanish theatre of forty years ago:

Quant à *l'entrada*, l'entrée, qui jadis était absolument dis-tincte de la place, elle n'existe plus que de nom, chaque place étant tarifée *con entrada* (avec l'entrée). Autrement dit, on n'a plus besoin que de prendre un seul billet au lieu de deux. Il est vrai que l'entrée donnait le droit de rester au parterre ou la galerie supérieure sans payer un sou de plus, ou de jeter un coup d'œil dans la salle avant d'aller prendre sa place définitive à un second bureau, mais on a simplifié les choses, et l'on entre au théâtre comme en France.[1]

To have paraphrased this statement, instead of giving it in the original, would have been to miss an interesting point. It will be readily noted that there is in it a curious echo of what Stephen Gosson wrote about the habits of the young bloods of London.

With the disappearance of the old complex system of admission Spain devised for herself another system re-markably in keeping with the proclivities of her playgoers; so much so, indeed, that no other independent country has seen reason to adopt it. Often to the stranger within the gate ignorant of Iberian idiosyncrasy it has proved perplexing. Writing of a visit paid by him to Spain some time in the eighteen-eighties, George R. Sims, the author of *The Lights o' London* and other plays, says:

I shall never forget my astonishment when, having wit-nessed the first act of a four-act play at the Teatro Reale in Madrid, I saw the audience changing before my eyes. There was a little, short man in the stall next to me when the curtain

[1] *Le Théâtre en Espagne* (1897), p. 17.

fell on Act I, and immediately a big, tall man took his place. The old lady who had been sitting in front of me was replaced by a young girl, and whichever way I looked I noticed a change in the audience. I was lost in bewilderment until an official came up to me and politely asked for my voucher. I showed him the one I came in with. "That is for the first act, señor." "Eh?" I exclaimed. "Is my ticket only good for *one act* then?" "Certainly, señor. If you wish to see the second act you must take a second ticket." "But I want to see the play through." "Then the Señor should have taken four tickets on entering."

I went out and purchased the tickets for the three remaining acts, and then I noticed that each ticket was a different colour. The first-act ticket had been white, the second was blue, the third was green, and the fourth was yellow. Between each act the audience was partially changed, and then the attendants came round and collected the tickets. I discovered afterwards that a Spaniard generally takes his dramatic fare in small doses, frequently seeing one act one night, another a few nights later, and so on. There is always a house waiting outside while the house 'inside' is having its 'turn.'

At some of the theatres a short opera will be played four times in one evening, and the audience will be completely changed each time. On Sundays, when there is a *matinée*, a piece is sometimes played eight times during the twelve hours. It was not until I appreciated this feature of Spanish theatrical entertainment that I could bring myself to believe a poster which announced the 7160th representation of *Le Gran Via*.[1]

Though here one finds the principle of sectional admission being applied to the older type of drama—for which it was not well adapted, but competition and its popularity compelled it now and again to be resorted to—it needs to observe that it was the uprise of the *género chico* in the revolutionary year of 1868 which gave the principle life and sustenance. The *género chico* has been defined by

[1] *The Era Almanack* for 1892, p. 76: "Some Theatrical Notes."

its able historian as "not, as most people hold, merely a one-act musical comedy (*zarzuela*), but any dramatic piece, with or without music, acted separately and not exceeding one hour in length." [1] At first farces and slight sketches were all the rage, but it was later preference for the *zarzuela* and its well-sustained vogue that led to the system of sectional admission becoming deeply rooted.

In the nineties so many of the Madrid theatres were successfully devoted to the performance of quartets of *zarzuelas* that the one or two houses giving the higher and longer type of play had difficulty in struggling along. The truth is that the system of sectional admission was eminently suited then to the social customs of the time and to the pockets of the people. To the man about town playgoing was a nightly, after-supper habit: the theatre was for him as much a place of meeting as a temple of the drama. Sectional admission meant for him that he could repair to the theatre at any time between half-past eight and eleven o'clock and, besides indulging in an hour's chat in the vestibule with his friends, see a one-act play for the trifling expenditure of a peseta, or, say, about eightpence of our money. Nothing if not the willing slave of my Lady Nicotine, he was permitted to smoke in the house during the *entr'actes*, and in the vestibule when he pleased. In some of the popular houses lounging was even encouraged. Automatic machines, such as one finds nowadays on the piers of our seaside resorts, were seductively planted in the vestibules. The man about town could go to his favourite theatre every night at the same time and yet see a different piece, as on each night the order of the four pieces played was varied. To elderly

[1] Marciano Zurita, *Historia del Género Chico* (1922).

folk also the system made prime appeal, for one could get a snack of cheap amusement and get to bed early. So, all things considered, it is not surprising that the *zarzuela* had a long-sustained vogue. Eventually, however, a change came over the spirit of the people, and its attractions paled before the iterated incursions of cosmopolitanism. As its historian puts it, the *género chico* died with the last mule-drawn tram-car. Intensity of racial expression had given way before the march of progress. *Hic jacet* was written in 1922.

Though, as has been said earlier, no other independent country adopted the principle of sectional admission, its working has not been wholly confined to the country of its origin. It was borne over to Cuba in the days when the island still remained a Spanish possession, and for long flourished there abundantly. Forty years ago there were in Havana, that gay Mabille of the West Indies, where life was taken easily, three or four theatres, including the Tacon, a vast and splendid opera-house, which were visited by Spanish and Italian companies, who gave their patrons a nightly change of bill. At one and all sectional admission obtained. One could secure a seat or a box for one act, two acts, or the entire performance, but usually seats were bought for a single act, at the conclusion of which the tickets were collected by ushers and the whole audience went out into the neighbouring parks and *cafés*. The most popular house was the Albisu, where one-act plays were the rule. Three audiences were entertained nightly, respectively at eight, nine, and ten o'clock, and the prices of admission ranged from fifteen cents to a dollar and a half. To the Iberian far from home it must have seemed the long arm of coincidence.

One must end, however, on the note on which one began, since the last word has not been said concerning the practice of charging the playgoer a separate entrance-fee. Italy has yet to come into the reckoning. It is difficult to know when the principle of the *biglietto d'ingresso* was first established there, viewing the fact that our earliest traces of it seem curiously belated. But it can at least be dated from the third decade of the seventeenth century, that epoch-marking period when the first opera-houses in Italy were erected in Venice. Most of these houses were built by subscription, and as a *quid pro quo* the subscribers were given private boxes in perpetuity, the whole theatre, irrespective of the ground floor, consisting of tier upon tier of private boxes—a nest, as it were, of magnified pigeon-holes. The owners of these boxes either occupied them personally or leased them out by the season to others. Seeing that there was nothing to prevent box-holders from inviting guests to share their enjoyment, the opera-houses soon came to be infested with deadheads, and by way of mitigating the evil it became customary to exact from all comers an entrance-fee of five Venetian lire, the price charged for seats on the ground floor. An exception was made in the case of gondoliers, who were admitted free, and allowed to sit in any unoccupied boxes. (There was an analogous custom in the London theatres of the post-Restoration period, in which liveried servants in attendance on their masters and mistresses were allowed admittance to the upper gallery.) At first, much as in Elizabethan England, the performers participated in the profits accruing from the takings at the door, but, this proving unsatisfactory, they were subsequently remunerated by salaries, and speculative sharing was abolished.

In this way, so far as Italy alone was concerned, Venice was instrumental in establishing a new type of theatre. The time-honoured open, amphitheatrical system was abandoned. As opera-house after opera-house came to be built in other cities, so the principle of the *biglietto d'ingresso* spread. In his description of the characteristics of La Scala in Milan in 1790, Saunders, after stating that the auditorium comprised six rows of boxes, with thirty-nine to the row, adds, " The greater part of these boxes are private property, and a small additional price is paid at every time of admission to see the performance." [1]

Century after century passed, but the queen city of the Adriatic still remained faithful to the principles she had inaugurated. In his book on Venetian life, written in 1880, we find W. D. Howells, the American novelist, saying:

A box does not cost a great deal, but as the theatre is carried on in Italy by two different managements—one of which receives the money for the boxes and seats and the other the fee of admission to the theatre—there is always the demand of the latter to be satisfied with nearly the same outlay as that for the box before you can reach your place. The pit is fitted up with seats, of course, but you do not sit down there without paying. So most Italians (who if they go at all go without ladies) and the poorer sort of Government officials stand; the orchestra seats are reserved for the officers of the garrison. The first row of boxes, which is on a level with the heads of people in the pit, is well enough, but rank and fashion take a loftier flight and sit in the second tier. [2]

Remarkable, is it not, that a theatrical custom in vogue in Elizabethan England should have persisted anywhere in the world down to our own times?

[1] George Saunders, *A Treatise on Theatres* (1790), p. 71.
[2] W. D. Howells, *Venetian Life* (Boston, 1880), p. 70.

CHAPTER IV

OLD-TIME REHEARSING

THE old maxim that one must go away from home to learn news of home, paradoxical as it sounds, not only is remarkably true, but has the widest possible application. Time and again it has been found to hold good in matters of historical investigation. The only contemporaneous record of the methods of rehearsing plays on our stage in Shakespeare's day occurs in the preface to *Speculum Æstheticum*, an adaptation for theatrical purposes of Tomkis's *Lingua, or The Combat of the Tongue and the Five Senses*, made by Johannes Rhenanus, an obscure German author, in 1613. Rhenanus is thought to have accompanied Prince Otto on his visit to England in 1611. Writing in his preface, he says:

> So far as actors are concerned, they, as I noticed in England, are daily instructed, as it were in a school, so that even the most eminent actors have to allow themselves to be instructed by the dramatists, which arrangement gives life and ornament to a well-written play, so that it is no wonder that the English players (I speak of the skilled ones) surpass and have the advantage of others.

That Rhenanus was not jumping at conclusions and deducing a common practice from an exceptional case is shown by the fact that Flecknoe, in his *Short Discourse of the English Stage*, published in 1664, after expatiating on the brilliance of the dramatists of the preceding era, adds:

> It was the happiness of the Actors of those Times to have such Poets as these to instruct them and write for them;

and no less of those Poets, to have such docile and excellent Actors to act their plays as a Field and Burbidge.

It is significant also to find John Aubrey writing of Ben Jonson that he "was never a good actor, but an excellent instructor." On the score of this evidence it may safely be predicated that almost until the end of his career Shakespeare rehearsed his own plays. To assume that every company in Elizabethan times had its own particular producer, as has so often been done by the unthinking, is to attribute to those times a specialization of function wholly uncharacteristic of the period. On the contrary, Elizabethan practice for long established the rule. Such was of old the tendency towards conservation of theatrical routine that the Elizabethan system of author-production maintained its sway until a period well within living memory. In the beginning it made for nothing but good, but in after-days, when the aristocratic amateur began to compete with the professional playwright for the laurels of dramatic authorship, defects crept in. When we recall that in the Shakespearian era plays were almost wholly written to order, and the main characters fitted to the capacity and idiosyncrasies of particular players, and also bear in mind that a considerable number of the popular dramatists were, or had been, players, it will at once become apparent that, in the conditions, the author himself was the best possible producer. Even in the nineteenth century, with Boucicault, T. W. Robertson, and Pinero to the fore, it proved an ideal combination.

In Shakespeare's day the rehearsals of a new play generally lasted about three weeks. It is not known for certain at what time they were held, but it is known for certain that in Restoration days they took place in the morning, and concluded considerably before three o'clock, the hour of performance. As acting in Elizabethan days was also an afternoon affair, the chances are that the Restoration players were simply carrying on the system of their predecessors. Initially there was a strictness in the holding of rehearsals not afterwards so rigorously maintained, or, if maintained, much resented by leading players of careless habit. It was the rule at the Fortune Theatre in 1614, and doubtless elsewhere in and about the same period, to fine all those who were dilatory in attendance. To arrive late was to be forfeited a shilling, and not to arrive at all was to be mulcted in double that amount. (This sounds trivial until one recalls that money then had at least eight or nine times its present purchasing-power.) Forfeits of this order were for long enforced in our theatres, and it is quaint to find them being complained of on occasion by leading players, whose offence was all the greater, inasmuch as their attendance was a prime necessity. In the course of a letter written to Garrick by Kitty Clive in 1765, objecting to certain deductions from her salary, that high-spirited and plain-spoken actress reverts to an old grievance, and reminds the much-plagued manager that "I had my money last year stopped at the beginning of the season for not coming to rehearse two parts that I could repeat in my sleep, and which must have cost me two guineas, besides the 'pleasure' of coming to town." That an actress of Kitty Clive's calibre could ignore the fact that rehearsing is necessarily an associative business, and not solely for individual perfecting, shows how little progress had then been made towards the attainment of harmonious team-work.

In Caroline times the better-class theatres had been invaded by the courtier-wit, who competed illegitimately with the professional dramatist by giving his plays to the players for nothing. His type abundantly recurred at the Restoration, and brought with it some abuses. Defective in technical knowledge, the aristocratic dilettante, in directing rehearsals, seldom knew exactly what he wanted, and he insisted on the maintenance of the author's right to distribute the parts, often to the grave disadvantage of his play. Nor was that all. To him must be attributed the long-existing custom of bringing a number of chattering outsiders to rehearsals, much to the darkening of counsel and the discomfort and humiliation of the players. This was the heavy price paid by the theatre for the services of the gentleman amateur.

All sorts and conditions of outsiders thus found their way behind the scenes. One morning in April 1713 Swift wended his way to Drury Lane to see his friend Addison rehearse *Cato*, and take his stand on the stage with divers other intruders. In writing to Stella concerning the visit he betrayed how little he knew about the conduct of theatrical business. He expresses surprise that the players should have required to be prompted repeatedly, and wonders why his friend the author should have taken the trouble to direct them. But it never struck him to ask himself what the devil he had to do in that galley.

So usual was it for the author to superintend the production of his own play (even when he was the veriest novice at the game) that Steele, when writing his preface to *The Conscious Lovers*, deemed it requisite to thank the expert who had done the work for him. "Mr Cibber's zeal for the work," he writes, "his care and application in instructing the actors, and altering the disposition of the scenes, when I was, through sickness, unable to cultivate such things myself, has been a very obliging favour and friendship to me." Steele, then, doubtless had competence as a producer, but the fate of many a new play might have been happier had its author been similarly afflicted. One of the results of inefficient directorship and the presence of busybodies was a prolonging of the period of rehearsal. What in 1600 was completed in three weeks in 1740 took five. But no theatrical manager had courage enough to bell the cat, and the lax, slipshod system went on and on. When Dodsley's *Cleone* was in preparation at Covent Garden in 1758 his friend Dr Johnson was among those who attended the rehearsals, and Miss Bellamy records in her memoirs how, when she came to repeat the words " Thou shalt not murder," he caught her roughly by the arm and interrupted with " It is a commandment, and must be spoken, ' Thou shalt *not* murder.' " One is not surprised to learn that the actress, who had not been introduced to the Leviathan, deeply resented this interference. What humiliations other players must have suffered when Johnson and several other of Goldsmith's friends buzzed around during the rehearsals of Goldy's two comedies may be left to the imagination.

Seldom fruitful of good results as was the old system of author-producer in the eighteenth century (though when the author happened to be an actor the story was different), it sometimes reacted in a very quaint way on the author himself. Owing to the fact that he was not *persona grata* with the public in 1769, at the time when his indifferent tragedy of *The Fatal Discovery* was about to be produced at Drury Lane, Home decided (somewhat unwillingly, at Garrick's entreaty) to bring out the play under a pseudonym, and persuaded an amiable young man of his acquaintance to do preliminary duty as the supposed author and superintend the rehearsals. The result was ludicrous. The foster-father of the play comported himself so clumsily and unconventionally at the rehearsals that it very soon became apparent that he was not the real parent. Ill-instructed how to play his unaccustomed *rôle*, he revealed the imposture by readily allowing the play to be altered, lopped, and corrected at the suggeston of all and sundry, meanwhile evincing a tranquillity that no mortal author could have felt.

Theatrical conditions ordained it in the old days that the player should seldom be long away from the theatre, since rehearsals were pretty constant. They were of two kinds, each with its own characteristics. Up to the Victorian period most theatres were conducted on the repertory system, short runs of new plays being interspersed with performances of well-worn classics and other plays from the stock. Consequently there was a fairly frequent change of bill. If the virgin play demanded (and at any rate got by prescription) author-production, the old play called for actor-production, the superintendence of some one versed in the traditions of the classics and the 'business' associated with the performance of old plays generally. In later life the great Betterton held this office, and was paid an extra £50 a year for teaching at rehearsals. A little later Wilks, the admired comedian, did duty in the same capacity at Drury Lane at a like emolument. After their day, whatever the reason, carelessness supervened. Writing in 1735 on contemporary theatrical affairs in *The Prompter*, Aaron Hill struck out at existing abuses, not the least of which, in his opinion, was the slovenly manner in which rehearsals were conducted:

> The prompter dispatches his boy to the green room to give notice when the lady or gentleman is waited for in the scene; then, in rush they, one after another, rumbling their parts as they run, hurrying with a ridiculous impatience till they have catch'd and beat back the cues; and then immediately forsaking the stage, as if they had nothing to do in the play but to parrot a sound without consequence. Hence those absurd insensibilities to the passions and distresses they are acting. Hence the want of that beautiful appearance of reality which should arise from their assumed concern in what relates to themselves or others.

Evidently from this the grave defect in early eighteenth-century acting was the lack of *ensemble*. Everybody played for his own hand. It is true that under Garrick this hit-or-miss system was largely abrogated, but the improvement was only temporary. Writing in 1775 in his book on *The Elements of Dramatic Criticism*, William Cooke complains of inadequate rehearsing, of " a lack of combined and easy action" and any " predetermination of the business of the scene," with the result that first-night performances were invariably crude, and so deficient in artistic co-operation that a handle was given to the chronic malcontents whose chief delight in life was to damn any and every play.

A score of years passed, and no great improvement was effected. When Colman, in 1796, published his famous play *The Iron Chest*, after its pronounced failure at Drury Lane, he made a ferocious attack on John Kemble in his ever-memorable preface. "I call the loved shade of Garrick to witness," he writes,

> that there never was one fair rehearsal of the play—never one rehearsal wherein one or two or more of the performers

very essential to the piece were not absent; and all the rehearsals which I attended were so slovenly and irregular that the ragged master of a theatrical barn might have blush'd for the want of discipline.

Boaden, Kemble's panegyrist, gives a somewhat different account of the fiasco, and states that, apart from Kemble's shortcomings in the leading character, failure was due to the extreme heaviness of the play and its intolerable length. "Its author," we are told, "was too ill to attend its rehearsals, and nobody would venture for him to cut away those excrescences which that very useful critic the stop-watch must necessarily have pointed out."

Then the surprising thing happened. Believing in his play, and not at all content to accept the adverse verdict pronounced upon it, Colman, who happened to be at the time manager of the little summer theatre in the Haymarket, submitted it again to the public at his own house, this time with Elliston in Kemble's original *rôle* of Sir Edward Mortimer. The result was that the play completely established itself, so much so that for close on half a century it remained a stock favourite in both town and country.

August Kotzebue draws a marked contrast between the systems of rehearsal followed at this period in France and in Germany:

A tous les avantages dont jouissent les acteurs français, il faut ajouter celui de n'avoir pas tant d'occupation que les comédiens allemands, parce qu'on n'exige pas si souvent des premiers des pièces nouvelles. Cependant il faut avouer que l'acteur français se donne deux fois plus de peine pour bien savoir son rôle. Il y a ordinairement trente répétitions, qui se font avec le plus grand ordre; en Allemagne, il n'y en a que deux ou trois. L'auteur est, s'il le veut, toujours présent. À la dernière répétition, quand même la pièce serait déjà

annoncée, il a le droit d'opposer son veto sur la représenta-
tion, et de déclarer que cela ne va pas comme il le désire,
et qu'il faut faire encore d'autres répétitions.[1]

The fact that the French were then taking such pains in
the preparation of plays accounts for their early and long-
unchallenged pre-eminence in matters of *ensemble*. It is
astonishing to find that the Germans remained content
with two or three rehearsals of a new play, until one recalls
that they never had more than a nodding acquaintance
with their parts, and during the performance had to be
continuously prompted by the bookholder. France ex-
cepted, carelessness of this order was then pretty general
in all the Continental theatres, but, owing to the fact that
with us the prompter was stationed in the wings, and not
at the front of the stage, it never made any headway in
our country.

Of the number of rehearsals given in London to a new
play at the dawn of the Victorian era we get an inkling
in a story told of Tom Cooke, the witty Irish orchestral
conductor, in connexion with the production of Lytton
Bulwer's play *Richelieu, or The Conspiracy*, by Macready at
Covent Garden in March 1839. On the morning of its
first performance one of the actors, who was wearied out
by the labours of preparation, said querulously, "We have
had no fewer than twenty rehearsals of this confounded
piece!" To which Cooke replied, "Then I wish you
luck at *vingt-et-un*." On that score, as it happened, no one
had any right to complain.

As manager of one of the great patent theatres Macready
so far signalized himself by extirpating one or two crying
evils that it is surprising to find him giving support to that

---

[1] *Souvenirs de Paris en 1804*, ii, 298.

old abuse, the encouragement of outsiders in the theatre during the hours of rehearsal. Having determined to bring his tenure of Covent Garden to a close with a striking, spectacular revival of *Henry V*, he began a series of arduous rehearsals of the play in April 1839, and, much to the annoyance of the players, invited a number of his notable friends—Dickens, Bulwer, Forster, Maclise, and others—again and again to attend. Forster, with his truculent, domineering manner, made himself especially disliked: he so far worked on the nerves of Mrs Humby, who was cast for Dame Quickly, that the words of her part kept escaping from her mind. The poor woman was as ignorant about Shakespeare's plays as Mrs Pritchard of old, and her comrades took advantage of her benighted state to persuade her to suffer Forster's interference on the ground that he was the author of the play! But not even her yielding to this amiable deception could induce her to tolerate his shocking habit every time she made a slip of shouting, " Put her through it again, Mac! Put her through it again! " The result was that she threw up her part, much to the loss of the play, a little known and vastly inferior actress having to be substituted.

CHAPTER V

ELIZABETHAN ACROBATS

ALTHOUGH tumbling and other feats of acrobatics had been seen and enjoyed in our country long before the rise of the Tudors, no particular impetus was given insularly to the practice of spectacular gymnastics until a clever troupe of Italian mimes and acrobats came to London in 1574, and so far succeeded in amusing good Queen Bess that she took them with her on her summer progress. To scandalize the Puritans in those days was to go half-way towards winning the popular suffrage, and when they came to give public performances the Italians gave deep offence to Zeal-of-the-land Busy and his congeners through having one or two female acrobats in their company. Little wonder that the masses were vastly intrigued by what the worthy Thomas Norton, in his complaint to the Lord Mayor, styled "the unchaste, shamelesse and unnaturall tomblinge of the Italian weomen." [1] Though the novelty was one not fated to arouse immediate emulation, such was the vogue of the foreign acrobats that it exercised a material influence on the arts of entertainment for over a quarter of a century. A year or two later, just as the first English theatres were being built, troupes of native acrobats sprang up like mushrooms. Time after time in the fifteen-eighties the Queen had the tumblers to Court at Christmas, enjoyed their feats, and rewarded them bounteously. For the

[1] Chambers, *The Elizabethan Stage*, ii, 262.

performance given by his troupe of eight at Windsor on New Year's Day, 1583, John Simons was paid £13 6s. 8d. (about equal to £100 of our present currency), besides being supplied with all necessaries, including gloves for all the performers. Gloves to an acrobat were surely more of a handicap than a help—the pun here is fully intended —but the etiquette of the times ordained it that every performer who appeared before the Queen should be gloved. It is noteworthy also that in those days narrow specialization of function was neither aimed at nor encouraged, and that even the tumbler had to be a man of divers accomplishments. On this very New Year's Day Simons' men had, among other things, to perform *matachins*, otherwise a series of intricate sword-dances in which combats were imitated.

With the increasing interest in acrobatics the Elizabethan players deemed it requisite to diversify their regular dramatic performances with interludes of vaulting and tumbling, but as the expense of maintaining a separate troupe of tumblers would have made serious inroads on their profits they went into training and became accomplished enough to do the work for themselves. One can readily approximate the period when this variety of fare was first given to the public by laying stress on the remarkable credit Stephen Gosson gives to the inspiring influence of the Devil in his *Plays confuted in Five Actions*, written early in 1582. "For the eye," we are told,

> besides the beautie of the houses and the stages, he sendeth in garish apparell, masques, vaulting, tumbling, dauncing of gigges, galiardes, moriscoes, hobby-horses, shewing of juggling castes—nothing forgot that might serve to set out the matter with pompe, or ravish the beholders with variety of pleasure.

To say so much is to impute that the Prince of Darkness was the *fons et origo* of the latter-day music-hall, for Gosson's enumeration includes its germs.

The best acrobats are caught young. By constant exercise the suppleness of youth can be retained until middle age. In 1585 the indefatigable Simons began training a troupe of boys "for tumbling and showing other feates of activities"; and before long he was travelling with them all over the country. To spend time and labour in this way without any definite and enforceable understanding would have been worse than foolish, and already youngsters were being apprenticed to tumbling, just as if it had been an ordinary trade or craft. A simile used by Dekker in *Lanthorne and Candlelight* (1608) helps to establish this:

> If his [the horse's] taile play the wag, and happen to whiske up and downe (which is a signe that he does his feates of Activitie like a *Tumbler's* prentice by compulsion and without taking pleasure in them) then shall you the *Horse-courser* laie about him like a thresher.

Remarkably enough, this practice, which sounds as whimsical as the misfortune which befell Frederick in *The Pirates of Penzance*, persisted until early in the last century. At the Westminster Sessions in May 1617 one Charles Presse, a merchant-tailor's son who had been apprenticed to Jacob Hall, the famous rope-dancer, "to learn the art of music, dancing, and vaulting on the ropes," was released from his indentures on his father's mendacious plea that Hall had gone abroad and deserted him. Afterwards, when the truth came out, the decree was cancelled, and a new order was immediately issued instructing that young Presse be released from his servitude to Hall and duly apprenticed "to some honest and lawful trade." [1] This, on the face of it, was an unjustifiable stigma, for, save in Gilbertian extravaganza, one cannot be legally bound to a dishonest and unlawful calling. Relative to the long persistence of the practice, it is said that James Green, the pantomimist, who died in 1881, and was otherwise notable as the father of Hawes Craven, the great scene-painter, was the last person to be apprenticed to tumbling.

Such was the early proficiency of the Elizabethan acrobats that in a few years they were able to challenge comparison with their foreign rivals. In 1583 an English acrobatic troupe sojourned for a time in Paris and Madrid. They blazed a trail which circumstances in after-years compelled many to follow. With the waning of the century England found herself in possession of more actor-acrobats than she could employ, and the surplus solved the problem by making long tours abroad. In Germany they won an especial popularity, but more by their vaulting and tumbling than by their acting, which was little understood. A passport given to one of these troupes in 1591 clearly indicates by the method of specifying their qualities that their play-acting when abroad was a minor business, since it describes its members as intending to " exercer leurs qualitez en faict de musique, agilitez et jouez de commedies, tragedies et histories." In the conditions music, as speaking a universal language, was naturally placed first, but its primacy serves now to recall the little-known fact that in sixteenth-century London the theatres had no separate orchestra, the players providing their own music.

[1] See *The Musical Antiquary* for April 1912, p. 178.

It is seriously to be doubted whether the most expert among living exponents of the art of ground and lofty tumbling have any right to pride themselves on their superiority to their remoter predecessors. Those who entertain any such idea may be commended to disabuse their minds by examining the illustrations in Tuccaro's *Exercer de Sauter et Voltiger*, an interesting manual published in Paris in 1599, and the first on its subject. Of the feats performed by an Italian tumbler at Kenilworth Castle before the Queen in July 1575 we have a quaint, if vivid, record,[1] but no such account has come down to us of the particular accomplishments of any of the English tumblers of the time. Now and again, however, when reading in the old dramatists, one gets revealing flashlights on their methods of procedure. Already they had availed themselves of the auxiliary services of the blundering clown. Macilente, in speaking of Brisk in the fourth act of Ben Jonson's Globe play of 1599, *Every Man out of his Humour*, says:

> He's like the zany to a tumbler,
> That tries tricks after him, to make men laugh.

References to the tumbler's small hoop, through which, with an eel-like suppleness, he contrived to squeeze himself, crop up occasionally. Being wound round with twisted ribbons, it was parti-coloured, like a barber's pole. Marvelling over the fact that he had fallen in love, Biron, in *Love's Labour's Lost*, says of " this senior-junior, giant-dwarf, Dan Cupid ":

> And I to be a corporal of his field,
> And wear his colours like a tumbler's hoop.

Fine scholar as he was, Hart, in his recension of the

---

[1] Furnivall, *Robert Laneham's Letter*, p. 18.

comedy in the Arden Shakespeare series, errs in maintaining that the reference here is to a hoop used for juggling with sticks, thus confusing two different kinds of entertainments. Though written considerably later, there is a passage in Fletcher's *The Noble Gentleman* which clearly shows what Biron was alluding to. Says Jaques in the second act:

> . . . there is no tumbler
> Runs through his hoop with more dexterity
> Than I about this business.

In that late Caroline comedy *The Antipodes* Brome indulges in a similitude which conjures up visions of the old acrobat while at his work. This crops up in the scene in the second act, where Letoy is giving advice to his actors. Turning to one of them in particular, he complains that

> When you have spoke, at end of every speech,
> Not minding the reply, you turn you round
> As Tumblers doe; when betwixt every feat
> They gather wind, by firking up their breeches.

It is somewhat of a puzzle to determine when the primeval actor-acrobat, as distinguished from the tumbler pure and simple, who, like the poor, has always been with us, ceased to be. The latest clue we get to his existence occurs in an interesting pamphlet published in 1616 under the title *The Rich Cabinet of Rare Gems*, in which we are told that the essential accomplishments of a good player are " dancing, activity, music, song, elocution, ability of body, memory, vigilancy, skill of weapon, pregnancy of wit, and such like." It is much to be doubted whether the postulated qualifications have been here enumerated in the order of their importance, but it is certain that in after-years few players had them all, save the Italian comedians who

MODEL OF THE FIRST GLOBE THEATRE

Designed by W. Noël Hills for the Shakespeare League, and now deposited in the Southwark Public Library.

established themselves in Paris at the end of the century. But what we specially need to note is that 'activity' was the term commonly applied to the acrobat's art, just as acting was known as 'the Quality.'

It is at any rate certain that the actor-acrobat did not survive the period of Puritan domination. One looks in vain for any trace of him in Restoration days. But the type recurred in distinctly minor degree early in the eighteenth century with John Rich's creation of the initial scheme of English pantomime. Though never again to be recognized as a general principle, it had in even later times noteworthy exemplification. Not to speak of lesser lights, Edmund Kean may be said to have belonged to that order. The man who could play Harlequin as well as he could play Hamlet was distinctly a reversion to type.

CHAPTER VI

AUTHORS AND THEIR FIRST NIGHTS

IN the last quarter of the sixteenth century, when plays were generally written to order and paid for either by lump sum or instalments before production, English dramatists had no cause for anxiety about the fortunes of their work. The players took all risks, but they kept themselves on the safe side by not giving more for a play than there was a reasonable chance of gaining recoupment for without delay. In the Elizabethan era all the world and his wife had a consuming desire to be present on the first day of a new piece, perhaps because it might also be the last, and they were anxious to be in at the kill; and the players took advantage of this perennial urge to get back what they had expended by doubling the prices of admission on that day. This they could very well do, as they took the precaution not to give more than from £6 to £8 for a play. If the piece succeeded it was profitable; if it failed there was no loss. But the terms proved too meagre for the dramatist, and the growing competition for the services of approved writers led early in the seventeenth century to their extension, something equivalent to an additional payment by results. About 1605, certainly not much later, besides the usual purchase-money, the author of a new play was given the profits of its second or third day, after the daily charges of the house had been deducted.[1] This was generally so material an enhance-

[1] Alwin Thaler, *Shakespere to Sheridan*, pp. 25–26.

ment of his pecuniary return that it created a personal anxiety regarding the fate of the play, and led to his secret attendance at the theatre on the day of its production.

But even in those earlier days, when there was no particular reason for perturbation, there was one sturdy dramatist who expended so much labour over his work and had so immense a belief in its importance that he was resolute enough not only to sit openly and conspicuously in the theatre during the first performance of his new plays, but (as if he were longing for the creation of that custom of author-calling which was as yet far distant) to come on to the stage at the end to angle for the compliments of his more understanding auditors. Light on this point is thrown by Dekker's retaliatory play *Satiromastix, or The Untrussing of the Humorous Poet,* as acted in 1601, wherein Jonson, as Horace, is made to swear in the last act that he will no longer commit certain offences:

> Moreover [says Sir Vaughan], you shall not sit in a gallery, when your comedies and enterludes have entred their actions, and there make vile and bad faces at everie lyne, to make gentlemen have an eye to you, and to make players afraide to take your part.
> Besides, you must forsweare to venter on the stage, when your play is ended, and to exchange curtezies and complements with gallants in the lordes roomes, to make all the house rise up in armes, and to cry that's Horace, that's he, that pennes and purges humours and diseases.

Whether or not this mordant rebuke taught rare old Ben to be less spectacular in his attendance at the playhouse, it certainly nipped in the bud any disposition on the part of other writers to emulate his example. There is an abundance of evidence to show that the dramatists of the first half of the seventeenth century were habituated to lurking in the tiring-house during the first performances of their plays, and that the audience assumed their presence, but not an inkling that any one of them ever came out into the open. To begin with we have Beaumont's quaint similitude in *The Woman Hater* (1607):

> There is no poet acquainted with more shakings and quakings towards the latter end of his new play, when he's in that case that he stands peeping between the curtains so fearfully, that a bottle of ale cannot be opened, but he thinks somebody hisses.

If, however, the poet's dreads proved groundless, should the pleading of the epilogue have been responded to by the welcome signification that the play had attained harbourage, the pleasure of the moment seldom ended there. Mayhap some devotee of the muses among the stage stool-holding gallants sought out the happy man and invited him to supper, or, if they were well satisfied with their bargain, perchance the feast was provided by the players. To one or other habit Ben Jonson makes humorous allusion in the tag-epilogue to *The Devil is an Ass* (1616):

> Thus the projector here is overthrown;
> But I have now a project of mine own,
> If it may pass, that no man would invite
> The poet from us, to sup forth to-night,
> If the play please. If it displeasant be,
> We do presume that no man will, nor we.

But in Caroline days, after the courtier-poet had emerged, there were some authors for whom the prospect of a free supper did not compensate for the imperfect privacy of the tiring-house, to which every stage stool-holder had ready access, and such as these preferred to await the verdict in another part of the house. Says the prologue to Davenant's *Love and Honour* (as produced at the Blackfriars in 1634):

> Troth, gentlemen, you must vouchsafe a while
> T'excuse my mirth, I cannot chuse but smile;
> And 'tis to think, how like a subtle spy
> Our poet waits below to heare his destiny:
> Just ith' entry as you passe, the place
> Where first you mention dislike or grace:
> Pray whisper softly that he may not heare;
> Or else such words as shall not blast his eare.[1]

Though a somewhat similar request was made previously in the epilogue to *The Captain* of Beaumont and Fletcher, one is doubtful whether pleadings in these old addresses are always to be taken seriously. The epilogue to Brome's *The English Moor* hints of the poet as usually skulking " behind the hangings, as afraid of a hard censure," and the epilogue to Glapthorne's *The Ladies' Priviledge* says that he is in the tiring-house. Shirley too conveys the impression that on his first days he was habituated to taking up the conventional lurking-place. The epilogue to *The Duke's Mistress*, as spoken at the Cockpit in 1636, says, " Venus deliver us! The poet stands listening behind the arras, to hear what will become of his play." Five years later, at the close of *The Cardinal*, when produced at the Blackfriars, Tom Pollard was pretendedly kicked on to the stage by the author to deliver the parting address, and retaliates for the scurvy treatment he has received by hoping that the audience will disperse without bestowing any applause on the play,

> And break his heart, or make him swear and rage;
> He'll write no more for the unhappy stage.
> But that's too much; so we should lose; faith, show it,
> And if you like his play, 'tis as well he know it.

[1] These lines have been derived from a collation of the quarto of 1649 with the text in the Davenant folio.

Shirley here wrote better than he knew: "the unhappy stage" was prophetic. Dark days were looming for the players. It is noteworthy that in the era then fast drawing to a close it had been customary on the revival of an old play to subject it to revision and alteration, and sometimes to act it under a new title. That a mere reviser should have been as anxious about the success of the tinkered piece as its author was originally sounds curious, but there is seeming evidence that this was at least once the case. When *The Lovers' Progress* of John Fletcher was revived in 1634, after having undergone revision by Massinger or another,[1] the epilogue intimated that:

> Still doubtful, and perplex'd too, whether he
> Hath done Fletcher right in this history,
> The poet sits within; since he must know it,
> He with respect, desires that you should shew it
> By some accustomed sign; if from our action,
> Or his endeavours, you meet satisfaction,
> With ours he hath his ends; we hope the best,
> To make that certainty in you doth rest.

These lines are characteristic of an age when the work of no dramatist, living or dead, was immune from sophistication.

A new type of theatre came in with the Restoration, and with it divers innovations, but the old order of things was not completely abrogated. Near the end of the century, at Drury Lane in 1693, when Mrs Barry delivered the epilogue to *The Old Bachelor*, Congreve's first play, she was made to ask:

> How say you, sparks? How do you stand affected?
> I swear, young Bayes within is so dejected,
> 'Twould grieve your hearts to see him; shall I call him?
> But then you Criticks would so maul him!

[1] *Cf.* E. H. C. Oliphant, *The Plays of Beaumont and Fletcher*, p. 241.

It would be rash to maintain purely on this evidence that the author's old habit of lurking on first days in the players' regions had been scrupulously followed since the King came to his own. It may be that some authors had already set a mild precedent for eighteenth-century custom in sitting during the performance in a side-box. When the Duke of Newcastle's comedy *The Humorous Lovers* was produced at the Lincoln's Inn Fields Theatre on March 28, 1667, his Grace was not present, but, to everybody's surprise, the Duchess acted as his deputy, and, as Pepys records, " at the end made her respects to the players from her box, and did give them thanks." Such a course is not likely to have been imitated, graceful as was the compliment, but it might have encouraged the hardier type of author to await the verdict more or less openly in a side-box. For this surmise some bolstering might be gained from the epilogue to Shadwell's *The Squire of Alsatia*, as spoken at Drury Lane in 1688:

> Ye mighty scowrers of the narrow Seas,
> Who suffer not a Bark to sail in peace,
> But with your Fire of Culverins ye roar.
> Bring 'em by th' Lee, and Rummidge all their store;
> Our Poet duck'd, and look'd as if dead,
> At every Shot that whistled o're his Head.
> Frequent Engagements ne're could make him bold,
> He sneak'd into a corner of the Hold.
> Since he submits, pray ease him of his fear,
> And with a joynt Applause bid him appear,
> Good Criticks don't insult and domineer.

All this, of course, was written playfully in anticipation, and it is by no means crystal clear where the author was supposed to be positioned. But it is difficult to see how shot could have whistled over his head unless he were in a side-box. The lines give the impression that that was the place normally occupied by authors on first days, and that in the event of a favourable reception they generally came to the front of the box and bowed their acknowledgments. If such was the practice a very close approach had already been made to author-calling, far off and all as that custom was.

In the conditions one would have thought that where the author was also an actor he would have taken upon himself the delivery of the epilogue, so that, in the event of the play's success, he might receive in person the gratulations of the audience. Yet there is a noteworthy instance where this course was carefully avoided. When Will Mountfort's play *The Injured Lovers* was produced at Drury Lane in 1688 he spoke the prologue (in which he made humorous reference to the fears of a dramatic novice), and left the delivery of the epilogue to Jevon. And in the epilogue the latter was made to acquaint the house:

> My brother Mountfort in the scene-room sits,
> To hear th' censure of your sharp, quick wits.

All is plain sailing, however, when we turn the corner and find ourselves in the new century. Writing to a friend of that historical occasion at Drury Lane, on April 14, 1713, when *Cato* was produced, Berkeley styled it " a most noble play," and added, " I was present with Mr Addison and two or three more friends, in a side-box, where we had a table and two or three flasks of burgundy and champagne, with which the Author (who is a sober man) thought it necessary to support his spirits." [1] What

---

[1] In view of this explicit statement one is forced to assume that Pope was referring to subsequent performances of the play when he wrote that " The numerous and violent claps of the Whig party on the one side of the theatre

was good enough for Addison afterwards proved for long good enough for other authors of both equal and less degree, though few found it necessary to summon up Dutch courage: the timorous lurked behind the scenes. On the *première* of *The Conscious Lovers* at Drury Lane in November 1722 Steele sat inconspicuously with a few friends in "Burton's box,"[1] a mysterious box so called situated in the centre of the middle gallery. It is rather startling to find that Macklin's prologue to Fielding's *The Wedding Day*, as spoken at the same theatre on the play's production in 1743, takes great liberties with the author, though assuming that he is sitting somewhere in the house, as if in a regulation author's box. Such a place, however, would have become too conspicuous for men of nervous temperament. Far from being of that order, Dr Johnson, when *Irene* came up for judgment in February 1749, tricked himself out in unwonted splendour, donning a scarlet waistcoat with rich gold lace and a gold-laced hat, and sat himself composedly in a side-box. In marked contrast to the phlegm he then exhibited was his friend Goldy's extreme trepidation on the first night of *She Stoops to Conquer*, which forced him to wander for long about the Mall, until he was persuaded by a solicitous friend, when the performance had reached the opening of the last act, to betake himself behind the scenes. While making his way to the green room he was much perturbed on hearing somebody hiss. "What's that?" he asked nervously of Colman, who was standing in the wings. "Psha, Doctor!" was the reply. "Don't be afraid of a

---

were echoed back by the Tories on the other; *while the author sweated behind the scenes* with concern to find their applause proceeding more from the hand than the head." Otherwise it is impossible to reconcile the two statements.

[1] Regarding which see Chapter XXII.

squib, when we have been sitting these two hours on a barrel of gunpowder!"

Meanwhile in France Voltaire-worship had succeeded, by dint of its eruptive enthusiasm, in establishing a custom which long remained peculiarly Gallic, but was fated to become eventually world-wide. This was the calling for the author at the close of an accepted new play. When *Mérope* was produced at the Théâtre-Français on February 20, 1743, the *parterre* was so inflamed by the superb acting of Mlle Dumesnil that it was moved by its transports to set up a loud-long cry for the author. Voltaire happened to be seated in a box with his old love, the Maréchale de Villars, and her daughter-in-law, and his response to this unprecedented honour was to rise smilingly and bow. But the enthusiasm of the *parterre* did not end there. Addressing Mme la Duchesse, the enraptured spectators begged that she would embrace the poet on their behalf—and embrace him she did! That established the custom, but with this difference, that future authors on receiving the compliment were expected to make their appearance on the stage. Naturally any happening of the sort provided some amusement for the stranger within the gate who chanced to be present. Robert Smith, father of the two brothers who wrote *The Rejected Addresses*, went to Paris on important legal business in August 1788, and fully recorded his experiences in his diary. After writing of his visit to Versailles on the 15th of the month he goes on to say:

In the afternoon of the following day we went to *Les Variétés Amusantes* in the Palais Royal. The entertainment was *L'Anglois à Paris* and *La Timide*. The latter was a new piece, and was so well received by the audience that the

instant the curtain dropped there was a universal cry throughout the house of " *L'Auteur! L'Auteur!* " The poor devil
of an author then made his appearance, conducted on the
stage by one of the performers. The clapping recom-
menced, the author made a most profound reverence to the
house, and seemed as if about to return his thanks for the
favourable reception of his piece, but his feelings over-
powered him. He clasped his hands together, then, opening
them, raised his arms above his head, and ran off the stage
without saying a word.[1]

Yet, though other birds of passage must have witnessed
similar sights in Paris before this, no one thought of
carrying the idea back for use in his own country. After
that memorable *Mérope* night a full quarter of a century
lapsed before the playgoers of any other nation began to
emulate French example. That Italy had not by 1771
adopted the custom she was eventually to abuse is a fact
brought home to us in Carlo Goldoni's entertaining
Memoirs.[2] Long after he had won his spurs as a dramatist
in his native country Goldoni settled in Paris and wrote a
comedy in French, *Le Bourru bienfaisant*, which met with
great success on its production at the Théâtre-Français in
November 1771. Concerning it, he writes:

On the first representation of my comedy I concealed myself, as I had always done in Italy, behind the curtain; I saw
nothing, but I heard my actors and the applause of the
public; I stalked backwards and forwards during the whole
time of the play, quickened my steps in passages of interest
and passion, satisfied with the actors, and echoing the
applause of the public.

At the conclusion of the play I heard clapping of hands
and shouts of applause without end. M. Dauberval, who

---

[1] Arthur Beavan, *James and Horace Smith* (1899), p. 56.
[2] In the case of a successful new play the custom in Italy early in the eighteenth
century was for the pleased audience, when the principal actor of the company
came on at the end to announce the next night's performance, to cry, "*Questa,
questa, questa* [' The same, the same, the same '] "; and the curtain then dropped.

was to conduct me to Fontainebleau, arrived. I imagined he came to urge my departure; but he came for a very different purpose. "Come, sir," said he, "you must exhibit yourself." "Exhibit myself! To whom?" "To the public, which calls for you." "No, no, friend. Let us take our departure with all expedition; I could not support it." Here M. le Kain and M. Brizard laid hold of me and dragged me on to the stage.

I had seen authors undergo a similar ceremony with courage; but I was not accustomed to it. In Italy poets are not called to appear on the stage for the purpose of being complimented by the audience; and I could not conceive how a man could, as it were, say tacitly to the spectators, "Here I am, gentlemen, ready for your applause."

After supporting for several seconds a situation of the greatest constraint and singularity I at last retired and crossed the stage to gain the coach which was waiting for me.

Some years later the shafts of ridicule were directed against the practice, but unavailingly. In 1783 an old afterpiece was played at the Comédie into which Dugazon, the actor, had dovetailed a rousing topical speech of his own writing relative to the truce which had just been declared between France and England. He very carefully arranged beforehand that some of his friends were to go to the *parterre* and call vigorously at the close for the 'author.' When the call was made Dugazon came on, and delighted the audience by giving an amusingly exaggerated imitation of the orthodox bearing of aspiring dramatists, who generally appeared on such occasions leaning heavily on a friend's shoulder, as if overcome with excitement, and with their features betraying conceit and affectation.

When the custom of the call at length reached England it was not, mark you, in an ordinary playhouse that it first manifested itself, but in a house of exotic entertainment. The event took place at the Italian opera-house in the Haymarket in January 1788 on the first night of Noverre's ballet of *Cupid and Psyche*. When the call came at the close Noverre was led on by Vestris and Mlle Hillisberg, and crowned with laurel by the dancers. The whole thing was too carefully stage-managed to wear the air of a spontaneous tribute, and it was deemed so un-English as to establish no precedent. For thirty years there were absolutely no calls. Then an epoch-marking innovation took place. At Drury Lane on December 3, 1818, the night of the *première* of Howard Payne's tragedy *Brutus, or The Fall of Tarquin*, Edmund Kean received the signal honour of a summons in front of the curtain at the end of the play. The distinction would better have been conferred upon the author had the audience really known, for Kean by no means felt complimented, and from first to last disliked the practice. But the strange thing was that while actor-calling became the fashion author-calling was long delayed. It is curious also to find that the Italian opera-house, after having pioneered the way, failed to follow its own precedent until 1824, when Rossini was director and composer there. Parke tells us in his *Musical Memoirs* that operatic calls first came into vogue in that year, and that Catalani was the first singer so honoured. Even so the summoning forth of composers to receive the congratulations of the audience was somewhat delayed. With us the first composer to be so honoured was Weber, and the occasion the first night of *Oberon* at Covent Garden on April 12, 1826. Weber was then a dying man, and he disliked the compliment equally with Goldoni and Edmund Kean. As soon as the cry was set up he turned to Charles Kemble, who was then managing the theatre, and said, " Mr Kemble, for why you make de people cry so for me?" And when told that he would have to go on it was with great difficulty that he could be induced to show himself at the wings. It was not until after he had tried to make Fawcett appear in his stead and take all the honours and failed that he reluctantly consented.

It is remarkable that theatrical history has failed to record who was the first English author to be favoured with a call. All we know for certain is that the call, if taken, was for long responded to by a silent bow from a private box, and that the now familiar practice of taking it on the stage came later, just as the author's habit of indulging in a few neat remarks came later still. But the chances are that Charles Dickens was the first English author—he was certainly one of the first—to receive in person the compliments of the audience. When Sheridan Knowles's play *Love* was produced at Covent Garden on November 2, 1839, he was loudly called for at the fall of the curtain, and *The Age*, in recording the fact, styles it a following of " a vulgar custom, first encouraged by Mr Dickens, and last by Sir E. Bulwer." Evidently author-calling had then been at most only a year or two in vogue. The Press did its best to stamp it out, but all to no purpose. When *Richelieu* was produced at Covent Garden in the March previous *The Times*, in reviewing the play, said, " Sir E. L. Bulwer, according to the new and most absurd fashion, being called for, made his bow from the stage box." Two years previously Dickens had three burlettas to his record—*The Village Coquettes*, *The Strange Gentleman*, and *Is She his Wife?*—all produced at the St James's Theatre. As the second and third were trivialities and unlikely to evoke any enthusiasm, the chances are that it was on December 6, 1836, that the popular author of *The Pickwick Papers* was honoured with a call at the close of *The Village Coquettes*, and paved the way for generations of future playwrights.

It is curious to note that when the romantic opera of *The Fairy Oak* was produced at Drury Lane on October 18, 1845, it was the author (Cope) who was called, and not the composer. Cope bowed his acknowledgments from a private box, a practice that was still being followed at the Olympic in 1853.[1] This later instance, however, was more of a relic than a continuance, for the latter-day practice had already emerged. When George Henry Lewes's tragedy *The Noble Heart* had its first London production (but not its first performance on any stage) at the Olympic on February 19, 1850, the call at the end was so imperative that the much-gratified author, we are told, " passed smiling across the stage."

[1] E. Fitzball, *Thirty-five Years of a Dramatic Author's Life*, pp. 131 and 259.

CHAPTER VII

PLAYHOUSE PRIGS

IN Scudéry's *La Comédie des comédiens* one of the characters is to be found saying that "the designation of thief is a term allied to the office of theatre doorkeeper, and an honest man in that calling is like the philosopher's stone, perpetual motion, or the quadrature of the circle—something that is possible, but is not likely to be found." If that pessimistic opinion was then universally held in the theatrical world, and remained unchanged for some generations, the rulers of that world had only themselves to blame for what measure of truth was attached to the concept. The crude methods of collecting entrance-money which so long obtained positively invited robbery. In the Bankside theatres of Shakespeare's day no one succeeded in devising any system of checking the receipts, with the result that the playgoer was allowed to pay his money direct to the doorkeeper and walk in. It is true that that worthy was provided with a locked box into which, through a convenient slit, he was expected to put all the cash received, but there were occasions when he somehow contrived to avoid doing his duty. Probably due to the mistaken impression that the female sex is honester than the male, women came to be employed to some considerable extent as ' gatherers,' but the pilfering went on all the same. In their powerlessness to cope with the evil the old players accepted the position philosophically, and joked over their losses. Do we not find

Dekker, in dedicating a play of his which they had produced to the Queen's Men, wishing them ever "a full audience and one honest doorkeeper"—as much as to say that they would be lucky if they could reckon on one.

Not even by the period of the Civil War and the closing of the playhouse—and that despite the fact that nearly three-quarters of a century of theatrical organization had been experienced—had any material improvement in the state of affairs taken place. In 1643 there was issued a mock lament entitled *The Actors' Remonstrance*, discussing the repressive enactments of Parliament, in which the much-harassed players are made to say:

> Our very doorekeepers, men and women, most grievously complaine that by this cessation they are robbed of the privilege of stealing from us with license; they cannot now, as in King Agamemnon's dayes, seeme to scratch their heads where they itch not, and drop shillings and half-crown pieces in at their collars.

When the monarchy was restored and the players joyously renewed activities a considerable betterment of the old system of admission took place. Tom Killigrew and Sir William Davenant, the rival patentees, put their heads together and determined that, in order to prevent the continuance of fraud, the check system should be introduced. This consisted of the issuing of what were called 'sealed tickets,' otherwise metal checks stamped with the name of the theatre and of the particular part of the house to which they admitted. No better method could have been hit upon to put a tally upon the takings, and all would have been well if the scheme had been carried out rigorously and without respect to persons.

Circumstances, however, arose which prevented its complete application. Let it have come how it may, a concession was simultaneously made to the public which led to infinite trouble. Playgoers had the option of seeing an act for nothing. If they didn't like the sample they could get their money back. Whether this was a foolish new idea or the renewal, under pressure, of an old privilege it would be difficult to say. One is inclined to think that it was a renewal, though no positive evidence can be advanced in support of that impression. It is true that money had been returned in Caroline days, but only, it would appear, when the vacillating playgoer left before the play began. Sundry references in old addresses prove as much, but no more. The prologue to *The Queen of Arragon*, a tragedy acted at the Blackfriars in 1640, opens with:

> Ere we begin, that no man may repent
> Two shillings and his time, the author sent
> The Prologue, with the errors of the play,
> That who will may take his money, and away.

So, too, the prologue to Cokayne's *The Tragedy of Ovid*, a play written about the same period, ends with:

> This said, you have our leave without offence,
> To take your money again, and go hence.

Whatever the origin of the Restoration privilege, it was for long availed of. Pepys, on occasion, found it most convenient: on one particular day he dropped in at both playhouses and stayed at neither. But the misfortune was that the gallants of the time who made the boxes their rendezvous thought the concession only half a concession if they first had the trouble of paying their money at the door, and their protests led to an arrangement whereby

OLD THEATRE CHECKS

the boxkeeper collected the admission money between the acts. This led to a good deal of fraud, as the wary, impecunious gallant—a type of which there were many—had only to keep shifting about to avoid payment. It was not, indeed, until 1745, when Garrick insisted that everybody coming to the boxes at Old Drury should take a ticket beforehand at an office provided for the purpose, that this trickery was wholly checked. In the meanwhile theatre managers ran the risk of a double loss, for not only were the gallants liable to dodge the boxkeeper, but the boxkeeper himself could not always be trusted to make an honest return. And just here one may pause to quote an appropriate anecdote from Davies's *Dramatic Miscellanies*, that mine of information published in 1784:

> Boxkeepers, whatever they may be now, by the managers keeping an eye over their conduct, were formerly richer than their masters. A remarkable instance of it I heard many years since. Colley Cibber had, in a prologue, or some part of a play, given such offence to a certain great man in power, that the playhouse, by order of the Lord Chamberlain, was shut up for some time, Cibber was arrested, and the damages laid at ten thousand pounds. Of this misfortune Booth and Wilks were talking very seriously at the playhouse in the presence of a Mr King, the boxkeeper, who asked if he could be of any service by offering to bail Cibber. "Why, you blockhead," said Wilks, "it is for ten thousand pounds." "I should be very sorry," said the boxkeeper, "if I could not be answerable for twice that sum." The managers stared at each other; and Booth said, with some emotion, to Wilks, "What have you and I been doing, Bob, all this time? A boxkeeper can buy us both."

But no boxkeeper could have amassed a tithe of ten thousand pounds by his pilferings, no matter what his term of office, and the story, as it stands, does rank injustice to King. He had other and honester means of making money.[1] An advertisement in the forty-third number of *The Guardian* shows that in 1713, besides being boxkeeper at Drury Lane, he was also mine host of the Punch Bowl, a tavern situated near the theatre. But, this apart, it is seriously to be doubted whether it was during the reign of Wilks, Booth, and Cibber that suspicion first began to be entertained regarding the probity of the genus boxkeeper. It may have been then, or it may have been earlier, that a scheme was put into execution to confound their knavish tricks. This was the creation of the office of 'the numberer,' a long-forgotten functionary about whom so little has been written that he deserves, and will shortly be given, a chapter to himself. It will suffice to say now that it was the numberer's business to see that the box-keeper collected all the money and rendered up all the money, and he effected this by sitting in a special box in the middle gallery and counting the occupants of the front and side boxes. Mostly he counted them separately, as at Drury Lane late in the seventeenth century (and probably elsewhere) there were two boxkeepers, each attending to his own section of the house.

The prime distinction between the Restoration money-takers generally and the money-takers of an earlier and a later period was that the latter contented themselves with robbing their employers, whereas the former were not averse to robbing the public. Even the wary Samuel Pepys was among their victims. In his diary-keeping days there was an institution known as " the Nursery," a crude

---

[1] To preclude temptation to fraud, the wages paid being small, it was usual to recruit the ranks of the boxkeepers from the tradesmen class. Plummer, one of the Drury Lane boxkeepers in and about 1744, kept a cheesemonger's shop in Kingsgate Street. Doubtless this practice explains the fact that when old Philip Palfreman, who had been for long a boxkeeper at Covent Garden, died at a very advanced age in 1768 he left a fortune of £10,000.

Academy of Dramatic Art, where recruits for the regular stage were trained and public performances were occasionally given. Of his first visit to this half-baked playhouse on February 24, 1668, Pepys records:

> Thence to the 'Change back again, leaving him, and took my wife and Deb. home, and there to dinner alone, and after dinner I took them to the Nursery, where none of us ever were before and the musique better than we looked for, and the acting not much worse, because I expected as bad as could be: and I was not much mistaken, for it was so. However I was pleased well to see it once, it being worth a man's seeing to discover the different understanding and ability of people, and the different growth of people's ability by practice. Their play was a bad one called *Jeronimo is Mad Again*, a tragedy. Here was some good company by us, who did make mighty sport at the folly of their acting, which I could not neither refrain from sometimes, though I was sorry for it. . . . I was prettily served this day at the playhouse door, where, giving six shillings into the fellow's hand for us three, the fellow by legerdemain did convey one away, and with so much grace faced me down, that, though I knew the contrary, yet I was overpowered by his so grave and serious demanding the other shilling, that I could not deny him, but was forced by myself to give it him.

The primitive check system had its defects, inasmuch as its purpose could be defeated by collusion between the money-taker and the doorkeeper, but it had so large a measure of usefulness that one is surprised to find how little it was resorted to in the early country theatres. Parke, the oboist, relates in his *Memoirs* that when he visited Cheltenham in 1800 he was introduced by Watson, the eccentric manager of the local theatre, to one of the minor members of his stock company in the following astonishing way: " Mr Parke, this is Mr D——y: he is the best-dressed man in my company, though he has one of the smallest salaries—but his wife takes the money at the pit door!"

Once the money-taker and the doorkeeper came to an understanding the only difficulty they experienced was how to bring about the return of, say, a dozen checks nightly to the place whence they were issued without anybody's being the wiser. The favourite solution of the problem a trifle over half a century ago had its own particular neatness. Every night at nine o'clock the pot-boy of the neighbouring tavern brought the check-maker by arrangement a foaming pint of porter by way of refreshment. When half of the contents of the tankard had been drained by him the boy was politely requested to take the remainder with his compliments down to the money-taker. An expert twist of the pot in the right hand of the finisher of the drink, followed by a rapid movement of the other hand over the lips, was all that was required to drain the contents and transfer from the mouth the dozen of thin metallic checks which had been dexterously dropped into the porter before it was sent on its last journey.

Naturally there were variants of this trick, and the business managers of the time did their best to render them inoperative. In the days before the introduction of stalls the boxes were the most expensive part of the house, and it was there that the check-taker was most watched. At the Olympic in the eighteen-forties the intending spectator, on paying his five shillings, was handed, not a small-sized check, but an immense wooden die, quite as much as a single hand could hold, which, on being dropped by the check-taker into his box, gave out by its sound an assuring indication that he had fully done his duty. The misfortune was, however, that these cubes were not only difficult to carry, but awkward to count, and after a few months their use was abandoned. A little later on managers reverted (quite unconsciously) to the old Elizabethan practice of placing women at the receipt of custom, an arrangement which for a time seemed to work satisfactorily; but when the sad and significant day came when two check-takers married two money-takers the bottom fell suddenly out of the device. It was not, indeed, until the late sixties, when Charles Calvert, the noted actor-manager of the Prince's Theatre, Manchester, invented and patented the ingenious contrivance known as "the Calvert Recorder," that anything material was done towards the abatement of regular playhouse thievery. But that was really only the beginning of the end: there still remained possibilities of leakage not readily to be detected.

What these were, and how they eventually came to be checked, has been revealed by Sir Charles Hawtrey in his entertaining autobiography entitled *The Truth at Last*. When that long-popular comedian was lessee of the Globe Theatre in 1884 he accidentally discovered that double tickets were being issued for stall seats in the slack season. Dates on tickets were then written in as purchased in the box-office, and the excuse was that mistakes in dating were sometimes made. Slips of the sort were always possible, but that was not the true explanation. Shortly after the boxkeeper resigned his job the theatre books were placed in the hands of an accountant. The clerk who had succeeded him had evidently been acting in collusion, as the accountant found that a great number of doubles had been issued for the immediate future, and that the box-office payments to the management were pounds short of the takings shown in the booking-sheets. So the clerk was sent to the right-about. Then Hawtrey and his brother began cudgelling their wits to devise a scientific scheme for the checking of accounts. They provided a separate bound book of tickets and counterfoils for each night, with the date, the number of the seat, and the part of the house printed on each ticket, thus doing away with the old system of date-writing, and making it impossible for duplicate tickets to be issued. The new idea spread like wildfire, and before long the Hawtrey system came into general use.

Remarkably enough, that was not the last time that Sir Charles Hawtrey had occasion to exercise his ingenuity to counter the activities of the playhouse prig. During his American tour in 1903 he arrived at a theatre in Texas, where he found to his surprise that the manager paid no wages to the attendants. On instituting inquiries he was told that the money-takers, a father and his son, owned an automobile, lived in the country, and were devout church-goers. When a real attraction came along they paid themselves for their services by letting a number of people into the house at reduced prices, giving no tickets and retaining the money, their appropriations on such occasions averaging about twelve dollars a night. Being forewarned, Hawtrey arranged that five members of his company should assist his manager in looking out for trickery. They had a very busy time, for some of the money-takers' old confederates tried to get in through the fire-escape, and, in all, there were quite a hundred people endeavouring to gain admission for ten cents apiece.

Times change, and managerial troubles change with them. We who love the theatre and heartily desire its

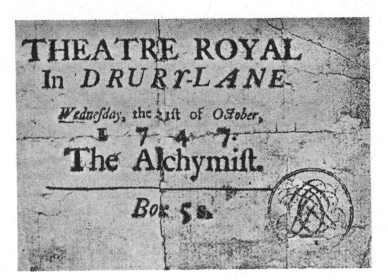

OLD BOX TICKET

well-being need not echo to the full what Thomas Heywood wrote in 1612, in his address to his fellow-players in his *Apology for Actors* : " So, wishing you judiciall audiences, honest poets, and true gatherers, I commit you all to the fulnesse of your best wishes." The gatherer of to-day has no option but to be true.

CHAPTER VIII

THE SHARING TABLE

MANY features of primitive theatrical finance surprise on first acquaintance, so different was the system rigidly pursued in the common Elizabethan theatres from anything practised now. In Shakespeare's day and for long after there was never any doubt as to when the ghost would walk. Everybody employed in the playhouse was paid daily. Remarkable as is that fact, it is equally remarkable that for one to be the recipient of regular wages was to occupy inferior status. None save the hirelings—a term which comprised both the minor players and the attendants—were paid in this way. The principal actors of the company, who were generally about ten in number, were remunerated by results—on the sharing system. After the daily charges of the house had been deducted—otherwise the wages and all the other working expenses—the receipts taken in certain parts of the house were divided among them, sometimes in equal proportions (as in the King's Company) and sometimes unequally. The receipts taken in the other parts fell to the theatre-owners, or 'housekeepers,' as they were called, who had much the best of the deal, inasmuch as they were responsible only for the upkeep of the building. The players had to provide their own plays, properties, and dresses, but they remained their property. With slight variation this system subsisted until the last decade of the seventeenth century.

Although the player of to-day looks askance at payment by results, and only accepts it as a *dernier ressort*, the old system was equitable enough, and, on the whole, worked out satisfactorily. To begin with, it obviated the necessity for much book-keeping. Simplicity was the note of the routine. Let it be recalled that there was no booking of seats in those days : it was a case of first come, first served. And until Davenant innovated in early Restoration days there were no checks to be issued or counted. Rich and poor alike paid their money direct to the gatherer standing at the door and walked in. At the end of the third act the gatherers deserted their posts and carried their money-boxes to the treasurer in his room in the tiring-house. Any belated playgoer who arrived then or later got in free. Hence the principle of gratuitous admission at the fourth act became well established, and held good until well-nigh the close of the seventeenth century, or the period when the taking of a second price was established. Quaintly enough, once the gatherers had surrendered their money-boxes to the treasurer they were made to do duty on the stage during the rest of the performance as supers—an illustration of the fact that in the Elizabethan theatre there was little specialization of function.

Once the treasurer had received all the takings he got busy. Since the receipts in different parts of the house had to be differently allocated he had to take care to keep them separate. From the players' portion of the money he first deducted the daily charges of the house, and then divided up the rest in shares for placing on the 'sharing table,' ready for distribution immediately after the performance. Regular playgoers came in time to know all about this system, and one finds a glancing allusion to it in the epilogue to Brome's Caroline comedy of *The English Moor, or The Mock Marriage*. There can be little doubt that it had been pursued from a very early period, possibly from the days when public acting was confined to the inn-yards, or some years before the first London theatre was erected. But it is not until 1605 that we get an inkling of its existence. In that year was published an anonymous pamphlet entitled *Ratseis Ghost*, in which a company of players is addressed in the following way:

> I pray you, quoth Ratsey, let me heare your musicke, for I have often gone to playes more for musicke sake than for action; for some of you, not content to do well, but striving to overdoe and go beyond yourselves, by S. George mar all; yet your poets take great paines to make your parts fit for your mouthes, though you gape never so wide. Othersome, I must needs confesse, are very wel deserving both for true action and faire delivery of speech, and yet, I warrant you, the very best have sometimes been content to goe home at night with fifteen pence share apeece.

In one respect the old sharing system was more comforting than the later system of remuneration by salary—'playhouse pay,' as the eighteenth-century phrase went—for 'playhouse play' meant that for every acting night the player was out of the bill a proportionate sum was deducted from his regular stipend. Remark what Compass says in the second act of Webster and Rowley's *A Cure for a Cuckold*, a popular comedy of the later Jacobean period: "There's better law amongst the players yet, for a fellow shall have his share though he do not play that day."

One must not run away with the idea that this system of daily payment was peculiar to our country. It was one of the old theatrical practices which had no geographical limitations. The French players pursued it. In Pierre Corneille's *L'Illusion comique*, an extravagant comedy of theatrical life produced at the Marais in 1636, there is an interesting epilogue whose characteristics are adequately revealed in the following stage direction: " On relève la toile et tous les comédiens paraissent avec leur portier; qui comptent de l'argent sur une table et en prennant chacun leur part."

Save that the French comedians had no 'housekeepers' to dig into their receipts, the French and English methods were practically identical. Chappuzeau, in his book on the contemporary French theatre, published at Lyons in 1674, says that it was customary after the nightly reckoning of the receipts and the deduction of expenses to distribute the balance forthwith among the players, according to their rank and numbers. Exactly how long this system obtained in France there is no means of determining, but it is known that it was still in existence there in 1720, and therefore lasted longer there than with us.

When the King came to his own again, and the players renewed activities after a dreary period of Puritanical restraint, the old routine was once more entered upon, and things went on for a spell much as if there had been no interruption. The terms of Sir William Davenant's formal agreement with his Salisbury Court company, drawn up in November 1660, show that the players continued to get daily dividends, and that the old sharing table once more came into service.[1] That the table and the methods it symbolized still remained in vogue a considerable number of years later is revealed in an interesting document of

[1] For which see Allardyce Nicoll, *A History of Restoration Drama*, p. 272, note 3.

December 1675 dealing with certain irregularities which had sprung up in the Theatre Royal, Bridges Street.[1]

But as the century waned a vital change came over the conduct of theatrical affairs, and this was to culminate in the loss of the players' birthright. It is a sad story, this, how the old sharing system disappeared. It begins with the union of the two companies in 1682, and the most of what ensued can be readily grasped from the graphic summary of events given in the anonymous *History of the Stage*, published by Miller in 1742:

> One only Theatre being now in possession of the whole Town, the united Patentees imposed hard terms upon the Actors; for the profits of acting were then divided into twenty Shares, ten of which went to the proprietors, and the other Moiety to the principal Actors, in such subdivisions as their different Merits might pretend to. These shares of the Patentees were promiscuously sold out to money-making persons called Adventurers, who, though entirely ignorant of Theatrical Affairs, were still admitted to a proportionate Vote in the Management of them; all particular encouragement to the Actors were by them, of consequence, looked upon as so many sums deducted from their private dividends. While therefore the Theatrical Hive had so many drones in it, the labouring Actors, sure, were under the greatest Discouragement, if not a direct state of oppression.

A revolt took place under Betterton in 1695, and, thanks to the King's sympathy with the players, a new theatre was established in Lincoln's Inn Fields. But this proved a mere flash in the pan: it delayed but could not avert the catastrophe which threatened. The spirit of commercialism had the last word. Little by little the adventurers encroached upon the preserves of the actor-sharers, until at last, early in the eighteenth century, they

[1] Nicoll, *op. cit.*, p. 291, note 2.

dispossessed them of their heritage. With Christopher Rich, the wily autocrat of Drury Lane, at the head of the offending all the players alike had to be content with a weekly stipend, and none too bounteous at that. By way of compensation for the meagreness of their wages and the irregularity of payment the principal members of the company were thrown the sop of an annual benefit. Degradation ensued. Not only had the players lost their long-enjoyed independence, but, through being forced to make direct appeal to the public for a measure of their subsistence, their self-respect. The benefit system was no more than a genteel moan for alms, and as long as it lasted the player had difficulty in looking his fellow-man squarely in the face. Not until it went by the board did he cease to be a pariah.

By a subtle irony of circumstance the old sharing system took refuge among the strollers, with whom, for generations, it remained a cardinal principle. In that respect Thomas Holcroft, the author of *The Road to Ruin*, who had himself figured in their ranks, hit the nail on the head when he said that "their code of laws seems to have existed, with little variation, since the days of Shakespeare." They alone were the final upholders of the old commonwealth principle.

CHAPTER IX

THE DAWN OF DRAMATIC CRITICISM

THOSE good folk who question the dramatic critic's right to exist, and are exceedingly sceptical about the utility of his office, seemingly overlook the fact that he is a natural emanation, that there were appraisers of his kidney long before there were newspapers, and that, properly considered, he is one of the inevitable manifestations of a higher civilization. To trace him to his source is to become convinced how difficult it is to organize public opinion, to teach people to understand that not all forms of amusement are merely pastime, that subjective impressions unassociated with some standard of judgment are worthless. It was not in Elizabethan England as in other countries, for with our forebears Aristotle had no rule, and in the absence of clear-cut, immutable laws the first rude beginnings of dramatic criticism were wholly devoid of science. Dramatic criticism then was no more than an idle sport in which all might indulge, and, like a good many other sports, it was fated to become professionalized. Most old sports had an element of cruelty, and this particular one was no exception. It was somewhat akin to bear-baiting. Sometimes it was a player and sometimes a dramatist that was tied to the stake. Primitive dramatic criticism was oral, immediate, irresponsible, unreflective, and, so far as it had any influence, destructive. This baiting, or the attitude of mind which inspired it, ranked high among the humiliations of the player's calling to which Shakespeare made bitter allusion in the Sonnets.

Like the arrogant Leviathan of a later era, the be-feathered gallant of the opening years of the seventeenth century who elected himself to membership of "the new-found Colledge of Criticks" and sat on the stage "to arraigne playes dayly" was fully of the opinion that Punch had no feelings, or at least had no moral right to have any. One recalls how Dekker, in his richly ironical instructions to the would-be man about town in *The Gul's Hornebooke*, tells him that:

> By sitting on the stage you may have a signed patent to engrosse the whole commodity of Censure; may lawfully presume to be a Girder; and stand at the helm to steer the passage of *scaenes*; yet no man shall once offer to hinder you from obtaining the title of an insolent, overweening Coxcombe.

Figures of speech are dangerous tools to handle, and even an expert craftsman like Dekker cuts himself occasionally. No section of the audience had an exclusive patent to express opinion. The Elizabethans so far detested monopolies, eagerly and all as they were sought for, that the last thing they would have conceded would have been the establishment of one in so democratic an institution as the playhouse. Had not Dekker already admitted that the place was Liberty Hall,

> allowing a stoole as well to the Farmers sonne as to your Templer: that your Stinkard has the self-same libertie to be there in his Tobacco-Fumes, which your sweet Courtier hath: and that your Car-man and Tinker claime as strong a voice in their suffrage, and sit to give judgment on the plaies life and death, as well as the prowdest *Momus* among the tribe of Critick.

Ragged and Tough had their own likings and dislikings and their own vigorous methods of expressing them.

They had the weight of numbers, and theirs was the power to turn down the thumb. Fenner's *Description of a Poet* reveals that, despite the opposition of the gentry, it was they who damned *Sejanus*. It is not surprising, therefore, to find that, while Dekker confined his satire to the stage stool-holders and the *alumni* of the College of Critics generally (some of whom preferred to sit in the twelvepenny room), Jonson was equally contemptuous regarding the judgment of both the classes and the masses. Nothing if not superior-minded, it was rare old Ben's misfortune to be given to the dangerous game of sneering openly at his public, and he played it once too often. In *The Case is Altered*, an early play of his, he makes Valentine say:

> But the sport is at a new play to observe the sway and variety of opinion that passeth it. A man shall have such a confused mixture of judgment poured out in the throng there as ridiculous as laughter itself. One says he likes not the writing, another likes not the plot, another not the playing; and sometimes a fellow that comes not there once in five years, at a Parliament time or so, will be as deep mired in censuring as the best, and swear by God's foot he would never stir his foot to see a hundred such as that is.

" The rude, barbarous crew," we are told, " having no brains, will hiss anything that mounts above their dull capacities." As for the pretentious wights belonging to the College of Critics, their conduct was much more reprehensible, inasmuch as they were not wholly devoid of understanding. " They have taken such a habit of dislike in all things that they will approve nothing, be it never so concerted or elaborate; but sit dispersed, making faces and spitting, wagging their upright ears, and cry ' Filthy, filthy.' " Yet, after all, it was this motley public, more composite and representative than any public has been since, which, despite its ill-judgment and conflict of opinion, inspired all that is greatest in our drama. It is true that there were one or two small select theatres, like the Blackfriars, where the prices of admission were higher and the audience was of a superior type, but the fare provided there was never better than the second best. Plays tried there were really heard *in camera*. It is the glory of *Hamlet*, *Macbeth*, *Othello*, and *The Alchemist* that they were sat in judgment upon by a common jury in an open court.

At a considerably later period, after the dilettanti had taken due revenge for his attacks upon them, Jonson, having gained renewed strength, like Antæus of old, by his bumpings on Mother Earth, returned with positive relish to the assault. When he framed *The Magnetic Lady* in Caroline days he had the audacity to bring upon the stage between the acts a couple of typical stool-holders, the one a man of sound common sense and the other a coxcomb of the prevailing finicking order. Damplay, who is all for the maintenance of the wits' old arbitrary privileges, is astounded to hear that the author was inconsiderate enough to think that gallants should come meekly to the play " and say nothing for their money." His *amour propre* is deeply wounded by his companion's opinion that in matters of judgment the professed critics were no better equipped than the ignorant groundlings whom they so much despised. But nothing that could be said would turn him from his purpose:

I care not for marking the play; I'll damn it, talk, and do that I came for. I will not have gentlemen lose their privilege, nor I myself my prerogative, for never an overgrown or superannuated poet of them all. He shall not give me the law; I will censure and be witty, and take my tobacco, and enjoy my Magna Charta of reprehension, as my predecessors have done before me.

Here Jonson wrote better than he knew: all unconsciously, he was prophesying his own downfall. But a little time was to pass before the Damplays of the hour were to silence him for ever.

Divers questions come uppermost and demand an answer as one ponders over these ebullient times. How, for example, did the Caroline dilettanti formulate their indictments? What were the *clichés*, if any, which most found favour? The best answer to these queries is to be found in the epilogue to Ford's tragedy *The Broken Heart*:

> Where noble judgments and clear eyes are fixed
> To grace endeavour, there sits truth, not mixed
> With ignorance: these censures may command
> Belief, which talk not till they understand.
> Yet some say, "This was flat," some, "Here the scene
> Fell from its height," another, that the mean
> Was "ill-observed," in such a growing passion
> As it transcended either state or fashion:
> Some few may cry, "'Twas pretty well," or so,
> "But——" and then stung in silence.

Time out of mind the dramatist's chief bugbear has been the parrot-cry of improbability. Aristotle ties himself into a knot in discussing the subject. Truth can always go one better than fiction, but the dramatist must avoid copying that 'one better,' since there are quite possible things that in the theatre won't be believed. He must confine himself to the law of averages, or risk condemnation. The Elizabethan era was distinctively the era of high romance, when imaginations were plastic and an improbable story could form the basis of a popular play; but it was an age of curious contradictions, inasmuch as while fundamental improbabilities were conceded (as in

The Merchant of Venice), incidental or culminating improbabilities were viewed as an offence. A charge of the sort was the only one to which Shakespeare ever deigned to make more than oblique reply. Apropos of the fooling of Malvolio in *Twelfth Night*, he goes out of his way to make Fabian remark in the third act, "If this were played upon a stage now, I could condemn it as an improbable fiction." A little later Beaumont and Fletcher indulged in a similar indirect retort, but not with equal cogency. There was one respect in which a good many of the Elizabethan dramatists, Shakespeare included, left themselves open to criticism. They were much too apt to maintain that the tintinnabulation of wedding-bells afforded a sovereign balm for hurt minds, and hastened at the end of their less serious plays to marry off as many of their characters as possible. At the suggestion of others people who had never evinced the slightest liking for each other clapped hands and made a bargain. Made conscious by rebuke of the absurdity of this convention, Beaumont and Fletcher strove to disarm criticism, when, as it would appear, out of bravado, they elected once more to follow it in writing *The Captain*. When, at the close of the play, Julio weds Cloro without conveying any inkling of his intention to his friend Angelo, Angelo, so far from expressing any surprise about the matter, merely says:

> If a marriage
> Should be thus slobber'd up in a play,
> Ere almost anybody had taken notice
> You were in love, the spectators would take it
> To be ridiculous.

And the spectators were in the right. It was not all folly that the stage stool-holders gave expression to: already the College of Critics had justified its foundation.

CHAPTER X

'GETTING THE BIRD'

IF it be true, as Dryden once asserted, that to clap and hiss when at the play are the privileges of the freeborn Englishman, then the time is ripe to note that for a good many years past the British public has been mercifully ceding one of its long-cherished rights. Happier in that respect than the bulk of their predecessors, the players of to-day so seldom 'get the bird' that one foresees the hour, none too distant, when the very meaning of that elliptic phrase will be forgotten in the theatrical world. History fails to record when the most sinister of all theatrical terms—most sinister, for, to the player, not even 'a frost' sounds more chilling—first came into vogue in its original and more understandable form, with the result that we are painfully ignorant of the identity of the genius who was ready-witted enough to apply to a once dreaded and not uncommon theatrical experience the classic legend of the alarmed geese which saved the Capitol by their cackling. If, in his hour of 'fluffing,' the bygone player got 'the Roman bird' there was at least the mental satisfaction in recalling that phrase that it was applicable in a *tu quoque* way to the persons who had indulged in the excoriating sibilance.

Many years ago Dutton Cook, in that once popular and still entertaining collection of reprints *A Book of the Play*, maintained that the old cant term "to be goosed" had its place in the theatrical argot of Shakespeare's day, but it is very much to be doubted if any such phrase was then in existence. Cook arrived at this conclusion on the principle of a straw showing how the wind is blowing, forgetting that the similes of the Elizabethan era betray the fact that the fickle wind was then for ever veering. Plausibly enough, he considered that he had clinched the argument when he quoted from the induction to Marston's *What you Will* the passage wherein it is asked if the poet's intention is to be "struck through with the blirt of a goose breath." Oddly enough, however, seeing how diligent he was in research, the strongest and most interesting item of evidence in favour of his contention eluded him. It occurs at the end of Porter's *The Two Angry Women of Abington*, that homely comedy which still exudes the odour of new-mown hay, and enjoyed great vogue with the Bankside audience of the fifteen-nineties. Sir Ralph invites the whole company to dinner, assuming that they will be content to take pot-luck—say, a bit of mutton or veal, possibly a duck or so, or a goose. This is Mall's cue for her speaking of the quaint tag-epilogue. Turning sick at the very mention of goose, she explains her qualms:

> Goose, said ye, sir? O, that same very name
> Hath in it much variety of shame.
> Of all the birds that ever yet was seen,
> I would not have them graze upon this green;
> I hope they will not, for this crop is poor,
> And they may pasture upon greater store;
> But yet 'tis pity that they let them pass,
> And like a common bite the Muse's grass.
> Yet this I fear: if Frank and I should kiss,
> Some creaking goose would chide us with a hiss.

She then goes on to describe the various kinds of hissing of which she has no dread, the calling "Hist, come hither," the hissing on of mutually snarling dogs, and what not, eventually coming to Hecuba:

> But 'tis a hiss, and I'll unlace my coat,
> For I should swoon sure, if I heard that note.
> And then green ginger for the green goose cries,
> Serves not the turn—I turned the whites of eyes.
> The *rosa solis* yet that makes me live
> Is favour that these gentlemen may give;
> But, if they be displeased, then pleased am I
> To yield myself a hissing death to die.

Conclusive as this may appear from Dutton Cook's standpoint, it is but an example of the veering of the wind. It would be idle to overlook what the speaker of the prologue to Porter's play had already said:

> Well, gentlemen, I cannot tell how to get your favours better than by desert; then the worse luck, or the worse wit, or somewhat, I shall not now deserve it. Well, then, I commit myself to my fortunes and your contents; contented to die if your severe judgments shall judge me to be stung to death with the adder's sting.

The truth is that in those days the two similes struggled for the mastery, but without any definite result. When their minds dwelt on hissing it was to thoughts of the serpent's tongue, and not to the goose's expirations, that Shakespeare and Ben Jonson reverted. It is curious that in their reflections upon the point a very common and familiar sound should have been superseded by a sound that few had ever heard, but the reason probably was that the adder's tongue was more suggestive, because of the deadly menace attached to it. One recalls that the Prologue in rare old Ben's *Every Man out of his Humour*, on being interrupted, refuses to finish his address, bluntly telling the audience, " An I do, let me die poisoned with some venomous hiss, and never look as high as the two-penny room again." Shakespeare, more deferential and conciliatory than Ben Jonson's stubborn, self-opinionated nature would ever allow him to be, could conclude one of his masterpieces with the ingratiating plea:

> Gentles, do not reprehend:
> If you pardon, we will mend.
> And, as I'm an honest Puck,
> If we have unearned luck
> Now to 'scape the serpent's tongue,
> We will make amends ere long.

It was a grave topic for either actor or author, yet Shakespeare, possibly because his withers were unwrung, could treat it lightly. When Holofernes and Armado, in *Love's Labour's Lost*, proceed to discuss the casting of "The Nine Worthies," and Holofernes objects to the assignment of Hercules to the page, on the count that he would be no bigger than the end of Hercules' club, Holofernes interrupts him with, " Shall I have audience? He shall present Hercules in minority: his enter and exit shall be strangling a snake; and I will have an apology for that purpose." This moves Moth to ejaculate, "An excellent device! so, if any of the audience hiss, you may cry, 'Well done, Hercules! now thou crushest the snake!' That is the way to make an offence gracious, though few have the grace to do it."

What William Fenner wrote in his *Description of a Poet* gives a graphic picture of the scurvy treatment given to Ben Jonson's *Sejanus* on its production at the Globe:

> But sweet Poesye
> Is oft convict, condem'd and judg'd to die
> Without just triall, by a multitude
> Whose judgments are illiterate, and rude.
> Witness *Sejanus*, whose approved worth,
> Sounds from the calme South to the freezing North,

And on the perfum'd wings of Zephyrus
In triumph mounts as farre as Æolus,
With more than human art it was bedewed,
Yet to the multitude it nothing shewed;
They screwed their scurvy jawes and look'd awry,
Like hissing snakes adjudging it to die;
When wits of gentry did applaud the same
With silver shouts of high lowd-sounding fame,
Whilst understanding grounded men contemn'd it,
And wanting wit (like fools to judge) condemn'd it.
Clapping or hissing is the only meane
That tries and searches out a well-writ Sceane—
So is it thought by *Ignoramus* crew.
But that good wits acknowledge's untrue;
The stinkards oft will hisse without a cause,
And for a baudy jest will give applause.

The truth is that no apt colloquialism dealing comprehensively with public disapprobation could have been rife in the Elizabethan tiring-house, since no one phrase could be made to apply to all the various ways in which the audience expressed its dissatisfaction. Though doubtless the most dreaded, hissing was only one of many methods of transient rebuke, even if we concede that it was the orthodox method of signifying a play's condemnation. Simply because heads counted, the fate of a new play depended upon those least competent to judge. That is why Shakespeare deemed it politic to throw sops to Cerberus. Not from Fenner alone, but from other and greater writers of his time, do we gain the impression that hissing was the prerogative of the stinkards in the yard and their congeners in the upper gallery, and that the gentlemen in the boxes and the gallants sitting on the stage rarely, if ever, trenched upon it. The evidence is cumulative, insidious. It begins with Casca's comparison in *Julius Cæsar*: " If the tag-rag people did not clap him and hiss him, according as he pleased and displeased them, as they use to do the players in the theatre, I am no true man." That the masses when at the play, and even before the play began, acted on impulse and were wholly without restraint is shown by Dekker's ironical instructions to the budding gallant in his *Gul's Hornebooke*. The gull is recommended to take his seat upon the stage before the prologue is spoken, and by his arrogant bearing to beat down "the mewes and hisses of the opposed rascality," otherwise those in the yard, whose view of the stage was more or less obstructed by the presence of himself and his fellows. Dekker goes on to say, "Neither are you to be hunted from thence, though the scarecrows in the yard hoot at you, hiss at you, spit at you, yea, throw dirt even in your teeth." One gleans from the same source that it was not apparently deemed good form for the feathered gallant to hiss, but that, all the same, he had his own particular methods of expressing ill-content with the fare provided. Dekker informs the nascent man about town that if it chance he fails to like the play or the company he finds himself in it is allowable to play the fool, to tickle his neighbour's ears slyly with a straw, "mew at passionate speeches, blare at merry, find fault with the music, whew at the children's action, whistle at the songs."

From all accounts the groundlings had no such gamut of objurgation, and, being incapable of nice distinctions, never made the punishment fit the crime. Taylor, the Water Poet, in his budget of rhymes entitled *Taylor's Revenge*, published in 1614, gives some graphic details of a riot that had recently taken place in that popular resort of the great unwashed, the Hope on the Bankside, and rapidly sketches in the various types of noisy playgoers.

Of one of them he says he " madly sits like bottle-ale and hisses," a description more than a trifle puzzling until one recalls that quaint simile in Beaumont's *The Woman Hater*:

> There is no poet acquainted with more shakings and quakings towards the latter end of his new play, when he's in that case that he stands peeping between the curtains so fearfully, that a bottle of ale cannot be opened, but he thinks somebody hisses.

But, as Taylor indicates, hissing, much as it was dreaded, was a comparatively mild form of old-time objurgation. The offending player had to be prepared to receive, if not precisely cavalry, something equally nerve-racking. Now and again, and more especially at holiday times, when a spirit of riot was in the air, the "understanding gentlemen of the yard" took with them into the playhouse a pouchful of stones, but if they chanced to be remiss in that respect they were apt in moments of stern resentment to tear the loam and laths off the walls and fling the fragments at the players.

CHAPTER XI

CALLING FOR TUNES

IT was a misfortune for themselves and, in some degree, for future ages that the Elizabethan players occupied a position of abject servility, and were compelled to gratify every whim which took their strong-minded public. How turbulent and imperious an Elizabethan audience could be on occasion has been well shown by Edmund Gayton in his *Pleasant Notes upon Don Quixote*. He tells us that:

Men come not to study at a Playhouse, but love such expressions and passages which with ease insinuate themselves into their capacities. . . . To them bring *Jack Drumm's* entertainment, *Green's Tu Quoque*, the *Devill of Edmunton*, and the like; or if it be on Holydayes, when Saylors, Watermen, Shoomakers, Butchers and Apprentices are at leisure, then it is good policy to amaze those violent spirits with some tearing Tragedy full of fights and skirmishes: as the *Guelphs* and *Guiblins*, *Greeks* and *Trojans*, or the *Three London Apprentices*, which commonly ends in six acts, the spectators frequently mounting the stage, and making a more bloody Catastrophe amongst themselves, than the Players did. I have known upon one of these *Festivals*, but especially at Shrove-tide, where the Players have been appointed, notwithstanding their bills to the contrary, to act what the major part of the company had a mind to; sometimes *Tamerlane*, sometimes *Jugurth*, sometimes the *Jew of Malta*, and sometimes parts of all these, and at last, none of the three taking, they were forc'd to undresse and put off their Tragick habits, and conclude the day with *The Merry Milkmaids*. And unlesse this were done, and the popular humour satisfied, as sometimes it so fortun'd, that the Players were refractory; the benches, the tiles, the laths, the stones, oranges, apples, nuts, flew about most liberally, and as there were Mechanicks of all professions, who fell every one to his trade, and dissolved a house in an instant, and made a ruine of a stately Fabrick.

It would be idle to assume that we have here a description of a typical Elizabethan audience, but it is certain that in striving to please a public more or less of this arbitrary order the unfortunate players made temporary concessions which developed into privileges and ended in becoming customs, not all of which were conducive to the general comfort, and at least one of which eventually proved a source of disturbance and discord in the theatre. This was the unseemly habit of calling for tunes. Strange to say, it was not the clamours of the *hoi polloi* that established this : in the beginning it was a class privilege. The custom arose in the small select theatres—known to their patrons, oddly enough, as 'the private houses'—where acting proceeded leisurely by artificial light and music was given in the intervals. It is impossible that it could have originated in the 'public' or common theatres during the first thirty years of their history, or within the period when the earliest traces of it are to be found. In them acting took place by natural light in the afternoon, and had to proceed with such dispatch that the act-intervals were of the briefest—little more than pauses. Moreover, until the Globe players (otherwise the King's Men) acquired possession of the Blackfriars in 1609 for winter use, and private-theatre procedure began to have some influence upon public-theatre routine, the common players had no separate body of musicians. When incidental music was required they provided it themselves. From about 1610 on there are traces of the playing of inter-act music in the common theatres, which would mean that, as the time of acting was still limited, as it was of yore, new plays had to be shorter, and old plays had to be cut down.

It will be recalled that when *The Knight of the Burning Pestle* was produced at the Whitefriars—a private house—in 1610 the Citizen and his Wife made their way from the pit to the stage, and, besides proceeding to direct the performance, indulged in conversation between the acts. Music and solo dancing were given in the intervals. At the close of the second act, when the fiddlers strike up, the Citizen calls for the playing of *Baloo* and his Wife for *Lachrymæ*, an indication of the fact that the calling for tunes was already customary, and that a conflict of opinion often arose regarding what should be played. Only one other reference to the existence of the practice in pre-Restoration times is to be found. When Shirley's Inns of Court masque *The Triumph of Peace* was produced at Whitehall in February 1634 Bulstrode Whitelocke super-intended the music. Writing on this score in his *Memorials of the English Affairs*, he tells us:

> I was so conversant with the musitians, and so willing to gain their favour, especially at this time, that I composed an aier myselfe, with the assistance of Mr Ives, and called it *Whitelocke's Coranto*; which being cried up, was first played publiquely by the Blackefryars Musicke, who were then esteemed the best of common musitians in London. Whenever I came to that house (as I did sometimes in those dayes, though not often) to see a play, the musitians would presently play *Whitelocke's Coranto*; and it was so often called for, that they would have it played twice or thrice of an afternoone.

With the Restoration there came in a new type of theatre, but, notwithstanding the break in theatrical routine occasioned by the silencing of the players during the period of Puritanical domination, there was a sturdy revival of old playgoing customs, with the calling for tunes among the number. This is pure assumption, since no end-of-the-century reference to the resuscitation of the practice occurs, but its prevalence early in the eighteenth century points to continuity and long persistence. In *The Universal Spectator* of June 11, 1743, is to be found an oblique satire on the theatre-haunting *beaux* of the times, ostensibly written by one of the brotherhood, in which the writer pats himself on the back for being the first to call for *The Black Joke*, and insist upon its being played. Later on Goldsmith took stock of the practice, and dealt with it quizzically in the twenty-first letter of "The Citizen of the World."

When given an inch the public of old was always disposed to take an ell. Since they were allowed on occasion to dictate what music should be played the gods saw no reason why their authority should not extend to other matters. For Mallet's masque of *Britannia*, when it was produced at Drury Lane in May 1755, Garrick wrote, and delivered in the character of a drunken sailor, a topically patriotic prologue which was so well liked that it was afterwards called for several times when the masque was not in the bill. To little Davy this proved more plague than profit, for the demand had to be complied with, and even on nights when he was not announced to act he had to attend and don the sailor's garb to be in readiness for the likely call.

Returning, however, to our subject proper, it is to be noted that although as a rule the tunes demanded were a matter of whim—so much so that rival calls were sometimes confusingly set up—there were occasions when the tunes asked for were curiously indicative of the general mood. At Drury Lane on January 25, 1763, where a large and highly resentful body of playgoers had assembled with the deliberate purpose of creating a disturbance over the prevailing prices of admission, the thunder in the air began to make itself manifest just a moment or so before the curtain rose. As if by common accord, sundry cries were given for the playing of *Britons strike Home* and *The Roast Beef of Old England*. There was in this a reminder that the rights and privileges of Britons were not to be tampered with, and although music is popularly supposed to have charms to soothe the savage breast it is not surprising to find that after the fiddlers had done their best there was some strenuous speechifying on both sides of the footlights, which so far added fuel to the fire that the proceedings terminated in a first-class riot.

Meanwhile in the Dublin Theatre—Ireland being much more prone to imitate England's vices than her virtues—the unfortunate musicians had been having a harrowing time of it. In the course of an interesting address made to his company by Thomas Sheridan, the actor-manager of old Smock Alley, at a period of theatrical crisis in March 1754, opportunity was taken to discuss how far it was expedient to comply with the whims and caprices of the playgoing public. After instancing a case of some perplexity Sheridan went on to say:

In such a situation the actors would be in a much worse condition than the musicians formerly were. We all know the dreadful usage they met with, in consequence of a claim of that nature from the galleries. They assumed a right of calling for what tunes they pleased, but, not always agreeing upon the tune, one party roared out for one, and the other was as clamorous for another. As the musicians could not possibly play both together they thought that playing them one after another would satisfy all parties, but that would not do. If they played the one the advocates for the other thought they had a right to precedence, and saluted them with a volley of apples and oranges. At last the outrage rose to such a height that they threw glass bottles and stones and cut several of the performers and broke their instruments. Then there was no resource found but that of ordering the band never to go into the box, but to play behind the scenes, at least till the pit was so full that they might be protected. This expedient, being often put in practice, put an end to the claim, and the band afterwards performed such pieces as were allotted to them without interruption.

But Sheridan was hugely mistaken in his belief that, so far as Dublin was concerned, the custom had been effectually squelched. There, and elsewhere in Ireland, it was fated to give trouble for generations to come. But what is remarkable is that when the nuisance was at its height no London or Dublin manager hit upon the expedient of establishing a fixed programme of music and notifying the public that beyond what was announced in the bill nothing else could be played. This would at least have relieved the musicians of the onus of responsibility, and afforded a reason for their refusal to respond to calls. But it may be that the old managers, knowing that 'the gods' seldom troubled to peruse playbills, thought that the expedient would have little efficacy. If so they were not far astray. American experience shows this. When the new Federal Street Theatre in Boston was opened in February 1794 the trustees of the house promulgated certain regulations for the better comfort of the public, either directly or through Colonel Tyler, their Master of the Ceremonies, and among these was the notification that:

The music will be assigned for each evening. It is therefore requested that no particular tunes may be called for by the

INTERIOR VIEW OF COVENT GARDEN THEATRE FROM THE BOXES, 1804

Showing the royal family seated in a left-hand box on the second tier.

From a print by Pugh in Harvard University Theatre Museum.

118

audience, as the compliance with such a request would destroy the arrangement, and, of course, cannot be attended to.

But American audiences had so long been habituated to call for favourite tunes (particularly *Yankee Doodle* and *Ça Ira*) that it proved difficult to make them abstain from the practice. To what extent the Boston 'gods' resented the new regulation can be gleaned from an advertisement issued within three weeks of the opening of the new theatre:

> The musicians that perform in the orchestra of the Boston Theatre assure the public that it is not more their duty than it is their wish to oblige in playing such tunes as are called for, but at the same time they wish them to consider the peculiar poignancy of insult to men not accustomed to it. Thus situated, they entreat a generous people so far to compassionate their feelings as to prevent the thoughtless, or ill-disposed, from throwing apples, stones, etc., into the orchestra, that while they eat the bread of industry in a free country, it may not be tinctured with the poison of humiliation.[1]

The reference here to a free country was distinctly unhappy, for freedom then signified the right to do as one gol-darned pleased. Elsewhere in the Union little attempt was made to stay the practice. Writing in 1803 of the public which then frequented the New York theatre, Washington Irving, under the pseudonym of Jonathan Oldstyle, says:

> I observed that every part of the house has its different deportment. The good folks of the gallery have all the trouble of ordering the music (their directions, however, are not more frequently followed than they deserve). The mode by which they issue their mandates is stamping, hissing, roaring, whistling, and, when the musicians are refractory, groaning in cadence.

[1] O. G. Sonneck, *Early Opera in America*, pp. 137–139.

But a bad habit can sometimes be put to a good use, and in Dublin the habit of calling for tunes once led to a highly impressive scene. On November 17, 1788, when a large audience had assembled at the Theatre Royal, Crow Street, to see Tom King, an old local stock-company favourite who had advanced to the dignity of a shooting star, in his fine characterization of Lord Ogleby in *The Clandestine Marriage*, news came to hand by packet just before the rising of the curtain of the grave state of the King's health. No sooner had the fiddlers trooped into the orchestra well than a general cry arose for *God save the King*, which was at once played, and, in the words of a contemporary journal, "instantly produced universal applause and abundant tears."

Considering how long she looked askance at the lures of the drama, Scotland fell astonishingly quickly in line in the matter of English playgoing customs, but came soon to repent her imitativeness. There was a glorious shindy—known to fame as the 'Culloden' riot—in the Edinburgh Theatre on April 17, 1749, when *The First Part of King Henry IV* was in the bill. In one of the intervals some Hanoverian officers in the house bawled to the fiddlers, bidding them play the air of *Culloden*, but were immediately countered by a demand from the civilian part of the audience for *You're Welcome, Charles Stuart*. Puzzled for a moment what to do, the band at length struck up the lively Jacobite air, whereupon the officers drew their swords, and, after chasing the musicians from their seats, climbed up triumphantly on to the stage. Always well provided with ammunition, the 'gods,' from the security of their fastness, assailed the raiders with showers of sticks and bottles, accompanied by many stinging execrations—all of which, as Dogberry would say, was most tolerable, and not to be endured. So the redcoats vanished from the danger-zone, and proceeded to rush up the gallery stairs with the view of administering condign punishment to their assailants. But, anticipating some such move, the gods had effectively barricaded the gallery door by piling up forms against it, and by the time the military got to the top they found themselves caught in a trap. Up behind them had come a sturdy phalanx of Highland chairmen, armed with sedan-chair poles, and bubbling over with indignation at the insult to Prince Charlie. Short and decisive was the encounter: hemmed in a corner, the arrogant Hanoverians, after receiving a few broken heads, deemed it politic to surrender. Next day, to prevent a repetition of the riot, the controllers of the theatre posted up a notice telling all and sundry that the musicians of the house had been instructed to ignore all demands from the audience for particular tunes, and play only what was set down for them.

It is noteworthy that, although by the end of the century the baneful old custom had fallen into desuetude in London, it still lingered in the provinces. Writing in his *Nine Years of an Actor's Life*, Robert Dyer tells of a personal experience at Bristol in July 1816, when he was on the threshold of life, and Edmund Kean was paying his first starring visit to that city:

> His first night at Bristol was an overflow. I went with a party, and paid box admission, but box places could not be obtained—we tried the pit, and were equally unsuccessful—and only by determination we at last obtained seats in the gallery, at box prices. I remember that on this day news had arrived of the surrender of the French capital to the Allies, and at the close of the play a cry was raised for the *Downfall*

of Paris. No attention was paid to the call by the orchestra, and the farce [?] of *Comus* began. The uproar was excessive. At last Bengough, who enacted Comus, addressed Loder, and a pause was gained. He told the audience that Mr Loder had said he did not know the tune called the *Downfall of Paris*, but if the audience pleased he would play *God save the King*. Leaders should in all cases of popular excitement obey a public call—it is dangerous to trifle with the many-headed monster; and though Mr Loder might not have heard of the *Downfall of Paris*, he surely must have heard of the *Battle of Prague*. I think, however, that the audience punished his refusal of *one* tune by making him play *two*—*God save the King* and *Rule, Britannia!* Musicians never like the performance of more than is set down for them.

Even if Loder had been acquainted with the demanded air it is difficult to know how his fiddlers could have played it on the spur of the moment without the music. In the old days perplexities of this order must have occasionally arisen. In Ireland trouble of another sort came with the frequent calling for party tunes, an abominable habit which introduced discord into the theatre and sometimes led to serious riot. When Thomas Ludford Bellamy, the noted bass vocalist, entered upon the management of the Belfast theatre in 1806 he grasped the nettle which had so often stung his predecessors by issuing the following notice:

To prevent any unpleasant consequences which may arise from airs being called for not advertised in the bills, Mr Bellamy deems it necessary to inform the public that *God save the King* will be performed by the band at the end of the fourth act of the play, *St Patrick's Day* prior to the farce, and *Rule, Britannia!* between the first and second acts, and on no account whatever will they be played at any other period of the evening.

Probably this made an end of the old practice in Northern Ireland, but in the south and on this particular

Pit Boxes & Gallery.

Etching by George Cruikshank.

score the gods did not cease from troubling for another forty years. How the nuisance eventually received its quietus is an interesting story. In November 1849 there was much excitement in Dublin City over the engagement at the Theatre Royal, Hawkins Street, of Catherine Hayes, the first native *prima donna*; and on Miss Hayes' second night, when *Norma* was in the bill, a loud demand was set up in the interval between the opera and the afterpiece for *Garryowen*. This was out of compliment to the gifted songstress, since *Garryowen* was a popular old Limerick war-tune, and the lady had been born in that city. There was no response, however, to the demand, and, the house remaining unsatisfied, the farce began amid deafening clamour. Finally Calcraft, the manager, made his appearance, but had great difficulty in gaining a hearing. When quiet was at length restored he began by saying:

"Ladies and gentlemen, it has uniformly been my endeavour to conduct this theatre with respectability and on a regular system. If the rules are departed from, if I permitted any portion of the audience to dictate to the orchestra what tunes they should play, if I once tolerated the introduction of a party tune (loud cries of 'It's not a party tune'), it would be impossible to know where the practice would stop. (Much interruption, and cries of 'We will have it!') No— you will not. You may tear the theatre to pieces, and you may throw me on the heap, but while I am manager, I will at all hazards maintain the established rules of the house, and not suffer the introduction of party tunes."

That, perhaps, was the pluckiest speech ever made in a theatre, and from the sensible-minded it elicited its meed of applause. But the malcontents in the gallery were not appeased, and the performance concluded amid general clamour. Nevertheless the courageous Calcraft had won the day. There was no more calling for tunes.

CHAPTER XII

THE BLACK-A-VISED STAGE VILLAIN

IT is more than passing strange that nobody has hitherto observed that a story told of Old Rowley on Thomas Betterton's authority by Colley Cibber, in his classic *Apology*, throws a revealing flashlight on the origin of a curious old stage convention, some relics of which subsisted until a time well within living memory. Once, when present at the Duke's Theatre at a performance of *Macbeth*, the swarthy King turned to one of the courtiers in attendance in his box just as the scene between Macbeth and the Two Murderers had ended and playfully asked, " Pray, what is the meaning that we never see a rogue in a play but Godsfish? They always clap on him a black periwig, when it is well known one of the greatest rogues in England always wears a fair one." As it happens, historians have been too much exercised in mind over the identity of the rogue in question—whether my lord Shaftesbury or another—to note the implications of Old Rowley's remark.

A little reflection must convince anybody of average understanding that the custom referred to cannot possibly have been of recent origin, else the Merry Monarch, easygoing and all as he was, would hardly have spoken of it so good-humouredly. Nothing but the stubborn authority of a long-established usage could have justified or condoned such a practice in the days when the restored Stuart matched his swarthiness with the blackest of black perukes, and was, moreover, a pretty frequent playgoer.

There are cogent reasons for believing that this assumed characteristic of unadulterated scoundrelism dated from Shakespeare's early days. If gentlemen even then preferred blondes they had no monopoly of the preference. An old, old dislike to dark-haired people was still persisting—a proof that they were greatly in the minority. As Shakespeare himself said in the Sonnets:

> In the old age black was not counted fair,
> Or if it were, it bore not beauty's name.

One recalls also that, love compelling him to run counter to the prejudices of the times, Biron maintained of Rosaline in *Love's Labour's Lost*:

> O, if in black my lady's brows be deck'd,
>   It mourns that painting and usurping hair
> Should ravish doters with a false aspect;
>   And therefore is she born to make black fair.

Shakespeare here betrays his poetic lineage: in this last line is an echo of a sonnet in Sidney's *Astrophel and Stella*:

> When Nature made her chief work—Stella's eyes;
> In colour black, why wrapt she beams so bright?
> Would she in beauty black, like painter wise,
> Frame daintiest lustre, mixed of shades and light?
> Or did she else that sober hue devise,
> In object best to knit and strength our sight?
> Lest if no veil these brave gleams did disguise,
> They sun-like should more dazzle than delight.
> Or would she her miraculous power show?
> That whereas black seems beauty's contrary:
> She even in black, doth make all beauties flow!
> But so and thus, she minding Love should be
> Placed ever there, gave him this mourning weed;
> To honour all their deaths, which for her bleed.

It must be taken, therefore, that the bestowal of a black wig and a dark visage upon the early stage villain was a concession to the bias of the times. It was in part necessitated by the circumstance that the Elizabethans liked to have all the characters in a play well and truly labelled. To have given a character called Black Will any redeemable qualities would have been viewed by them as a gross and punishable deception; and, as a matter of fact, the Black Will of *Arden of Feversham* has none. Stage villains were expected to lose no time in showing their hands, and the vogue of soliloquy readily enabled them to reveal their innermost thoughts. Attire was distinguishing, and often symbolic. Kings seldom appeared without their crowns, and the King in the dumb show in *Hamlet* actually lay down and went to sleep in his. Hence the prime utility of the coal-black wig. Once a player emerged wearing one the spectator became assured that nefariousness was in the air and about to get in its deadly work. It takes all sorts to make an audience, and in this way things were made easy for the obtuse.

All this has something more than mere likelihood to recommend it. One can advance a modicum of supporting evidence. That the theory may not go ignobly by the board the irrepressible Tom Killigrew comes timely to the rescue. Fated as patentee of the King's Company to figure prominently in the complex story of the Restoration theatre, Killigrew had early dramatic aspirations never wholly to be gratified, though he had the good fortune at the outset of his career to have two plays produced in later Caroline days at the Cockpit. Too uncompromising a royalist to find comfort in his own country in the *interregnum*, he spent some years quite agreeably on the Continent. In the winter of 1649, while sojourning now at Turin and now at Florence as Charles II's ambassador, he employed his leisure in writing a tragi-comedy in two parts, based on a popular French romance, and entitled *Cicilia and Clorinda*, which play, though it was apparently never put on the boards, managed to get into print in London in 1663. From the present point of view its preservation was nothing short of a stroke of good luck, inasmuch as that, relative to the attire of the villain of the piece, one reads in the book: "Orante is cloathed in black, with black feathers, black periwig, his person crooked and ugly, with a dagger by his side."

On the whole, then, there are pretty good reasons for believing that the stage convention against which Old Rowley so quaintly protested had had its origin consider-ably before his day, and it is certain that it persisted long after. One recalls how in 1709, at a time when much internal commotion was taking place at Drury Lane, Steele announced in *The Tatler* a pretended sale of the theatre's effects, of which he gave a humorous list, including "the Complexion of a Murderer in a Bandbox; consisting of a large Piece of burnt Cork, and a Coal-black Peruke." Time passes, but the story remains the same. In his poem of *The Actor*, written in 1762, Robert Lloyd inveighs against the monotonous stability of theatrical costume thuswise:

> To suit the dress demands the actor's art,
> Yet some there are who overdress the part.
> To some prescriptive right gives settled things—
> Black wigs to murderers, feathered hats to kings.
> Yet Michael Cassio might be drunk enough,
> Though all his features were not grimed in snuff.
> Why should Poll Peachum shine in satin clothes?
> Why every devil dance in scarlet hose?

Garrick had thoughts of reforming all this, but he

eventually confessed that his hand had been stayed by a dread of the inevitable protests of the conservative-minded occupants of the galleries, more particularly since such protests usually took the form of bottles and rotten apples. So progress was slow. In this connexion it is noteworthy that Tom Davies, the actor-bookseller and Garrick's quondam associate, takes occasion in his *Dramatic Miscellanies*, published in 1784, to put an untenable gloss upon Hamlet's outburst, " Begin, murderer . . . leave thy damnable faces, and begin." To his mind:

> This contains a censure upon the custom of certain actors, who were cast into the parts of conspirators, traitors and murderers, who used to disguise themselves in very black wigs, and distort their features in order to appear terrible; in short, to discover that which art should teach them to conceal. I have seen Hippisley act the first Murderer in *Macbeth*; his face was made pale with chalk, distinguished with large whiskers, and a long black wig. This custom of dressing so preposterously the hateful implements of the tragic scene is now almost worn out.

It would be making a grave mistake to conclude from Davies' final expression of opinion that the black-a-vised stage villain was about to receive his quietus.[1] Neither he nor any other person of his time could have foreseen the imminent rise of melodrama, that new dramatic delight which was fated either to prolong the existence of or resuscitate (one hardly knows which) the hoary convention. Beginning in an atmosphere of rich romanticism and ending in one of lurid realism, melodrama, through-

---

[1] Even as he wrote elsewhere than in London the old symbolism was dying hard. John Bernard tells us in his *Retrospections of the Stage* that at Dublin in 1782 a player named Barrett, when acting Glenalvon in the old tragedy of *Douglas*—one of those self-communing, self-revealing villains of the Iago order—" was dressed in an entire suit of black, with a black wig, and a black velvet hat crowned with an immense plume of black feathers, which, bending before him, gave him very much the aspect of a mourning coach-horse."

out all its mutatition hugged the black-browed villain to
its heart. Vainly did a stray iconoclast rebel. With some
vividness do I recall that forty-odd years ago there was
a fertile-minded actor-author touring the provinces with
his own well-knit melodramas, one F. A. Scudamore by
name, who conceived the idea that the public was aweary
of dark-complexioned miscreants, and wrote a piece in
which the bright particular villain was flaxen-haired. But
the novelty, so far from affording any intellectual refreshment, was viewed as an outrage on the law and the
prophets. For some few remaining years the villain still
pursued her, but it was the black-a-vised villain of old.

CHAPTER XIII

THE OLD CANDLESNUFFER

THEATRICAL conditions in bygone times necessitated many rupturings of stage illusion which, through sheer usage, came to be taken as a matter of course, though none of them would now be deemed tolerable. Scenery was moved in sight, and liveried attendants came on now and then to remove tables and chairs. Until he himself was snuffed out by the universal employment of gas, the candlesnuffer had perforce to obtrude himself in the midst of the traffic of the scene to fulfil his humble office. Guttering tallow dips called for immediate attention. His was the distinction to be the first individual in the theatre to receive a call, but it was a necessary, not a complimentary, summoning. When the stage lights began to flare or flicker out the gods commonly set up a cry of " Snuffers! Snuffers! " foreseeing a happy opportunity of indulging in some facetiousness at that worthy's expense—*badinage*, however, which, as he went deftly about his work, was generally received by him with the utmost aplomb. A story told by Henry Fielding in *The True Patriot* in 1746 clearly indicates that speed was the main essential of the old candlesnuffer's office:

> I knew a gentleman who had a great delight in observing the humours of the vulgar, and for that purpose used frequently to mount into the upper gallery. Here, as he told me, he once seated himself between two persons, one of whom he soon discovered to be a broken tailor and the other a servant in a country family just arrived in town. The play

was *Henry the Eighth*, with that august representation of the coronation. The former of these, instead of admiring the great magnificence exhibited in that ceremony, observed with a sigh " that he believed very few of those clothes were paid for." And the latter, being asked how he liked the play (being the first he had ever seen), answered, " It was all very fine "; but nothing came up, in his opinion, to the ingenuity of snuffing the candles.

A familiar in the playhouse even in Burbage's earliest days, and remaining so until Edmund Kean disappeared from the boards, the old candlesnuffer had a remarkably long innings. It is true that in the common Elizabethan theatres, with their open roofs and natural lighting, he never gained any foothold, but in the small select theatres of the time his presence proved imperative. As a matter of fact, it is in connexion with these so-called 'private houses'—a misleading term, since they were anything but private—that we first learn of his existence. When that old play of disputed authorship *The Careless Shepherdess* was revived at Salisbury Court in 1638, by way of extra attraction it was provided with a brand-new topical induction in which four people typical of both town and country life were shown in the act of entering the play-house. Thrift, the citizen, on encountering Sparke, the Inns of Court gentleman, asks him:

> Sir, was't a Poet or a Gentleman
> That writ this play? The Court, and Inns of Court,
> Of late bring forth more wit than all the Taverns,
> Which makes me pity playwrights; they were poor
> Before, even to a proverb; now their trade
> Must needs go down, when so many set up.
> I do not think but I shall shortly see
> One poet sue to keep the door, another
> To be prompter, a third to snuff the candles.
> Pray, sir, has any gentleman of late
> Begg'd the monopoly of comedies?

With the Restoration invidious distinctions in the matter of theatres disappeared. No house was then styled private, and all playgoers had the shelter of a roof. There was but one class of theatre, and to it the candle-snuffer was transferred. This is pure deduction, though based on sound premises: it is not until near the end of the century that we gain any positive evidence of his persistence. In 1691 there was issued a pamphlet entitled *Wit for Money*, written in dialogue form and satirizing Tom D'Urfey the dramatist. In it Stutter (otherwise D'Urfey) is made to say that he is chary of giving vent to his wit when in the presence of the players: "Gad, tho' it were but before the Candlesnuffer, I dare not utter one good word—who can tell but he hath a play upon the stocks, and ready to be launch'd next Term?"

In the candlelighting era England, of course, had no monopoly of the snuffer. He was ubiquitous: wherever a theatre was, there was he. If no candlesnuffer by occupation is known to have written a play, at least one dramatist is known to have fulfilled the office of candlesnuffer. When the itinerant French comedians of the seventeenth century took a dramatic poet in their train they treated him with scant respect, and expected him to make himself generally useful. Once upon a time Ragueneau, of versatile memory, went on tour with Molière's company, and found himself assigned the humiliating office of trimming the lights. Writing in 1674 of the Paris theatres of the time, Chappuzeau informs us that the scene-painter of the house either performed the candlesnuffing or had it done under his authority. It was his perquisite to obtain the candle-ends left at the close of the performance.

By way of compensation for the humbleness of his

office and the insults hurled at his unoffending head, literature and the drama have embalmed the memory of the old functionary. One recalls how Goldsmith's Strolling Player took pride in relating how he began at the foot of the ladder. "I snuffed the candles; and let me tell you, that without a candlesnuffer the piece would lose half its embellishment." One day he got his chance: one of the players fell ill, and, as a desperate resource, it was decided that he should take his place. "I learnt my part," he goes on to say, "with astonishing rapidity, and bade adieu to snuffing candles for ever. I found that nature had designed me for more noble employment, and I was resolved to take her when in the humour." In this there may have been a reminiscence of John Hippisley the comedian's early experience. Hippisley began life as a candlesnuffer, and while following that occupation received a severe, if lucky, burn, which left a permanent scar on his face—lucky because it grotesquely accentuated the humorous appeal of his face-making. Once, when somebody told Quin, the witty tragedian, that Hippisley's son was thinking of taking to the boards, his only comment was "Then we must burn him without delay."

It is interesting to note that when Foote brought out his comedy of *The Orators* at the Haymarket in 1762 he made the theatre candlesnuffer one of the characters in the prelude, and gave him a few words to say; but history does not record whether the part was played by the real candlesnuffer or by some player who aped him. Evidently no one had taken more stock of the harmless, necessary light-trimmer while he was engaged at his work than the modern Aristophanes. In his earlier comedy *The Minor* there is a character called Shift, who gives an amusing account of his former experiences. From being a linkboy outside a country playhouse he found himself promoted to a post within. "I did the honours," he says,

> of the barn by sweeping the stage and clipping the candles. Here my skill and address were so conspicuous that it procured me the same office the ensuing winter at Drury Lane, where I acquired intrepidity, the crown of all my virtues.

The work, in his opinion, demanded some nerve,

> for I think, sir, that he who dare stand the shot of the gallery, in lighting and sweeping, the first night of a new play, may bid defiance to the pillory, with all its customary compliments.

Then comes a happy satirical allusion to the recent riots at Old Drury over the employment of foreign dancers in the spectacle of *The Chinese Festival*:

> But an unlucky crab-apple, applied to my right eye by a patriot gingerbread baker from the Borough who would not suffer three dancers from Switzerland because he hated the French, forced me to a precipitate retreat.

Since the old candlesnuffer had a good deal of idle time on his hands, and a narrow economy ruled in our early theatres, it is not surprising to find that he was pressed into service now and again as a super. One is by no means disposed to advance as evidence on this score Addison's story in an early number of *The Spectator* of the candlesnuffer who played the part of a fighting lion in an Italian opera at the Haymarket. Much that is plausibly related in these humorous old essays is pure fiction. All that one can say with safety is that the thing might have happened. It is pretty certain that even in Queen Anne's day the candlesnuffer made occasional appearances on the stage in another capacity besides his normal one. But positive proof lingers until a later era. In an anonymous satirical poem on "The Playhouse," published in *The Royal Magazine* in 1766, we read that

> The Prince then enters on the stage in state;
> Behind a guard of candlesnuffers wait.

Here the plurality expressed somewhat surprises, but, admitting that the guard was small, it is strictly in order. There has happily come down to us a theatrical document drafted in London in 1705, and in this it is revealed that two candlesnuffers were regularly employed. It is true that, as in the French theatres of an earlier period, one confined his attention to the stage lights and the other to the lights in the auditorium, but this is nothing against the occasional employment of both as supers. As a matter of fact, both figured in their dual capacities until the end of the century. A correspondent signing himself "Theatricus" writes to *The Monthly Mirror* of November 1797, complaining that in the funeral dirge in the recent revival of Garrick's version of *Romeo and Juliet* the chief mourners were inefficiently represented by a motley array of candlesnuffers and scene-shifters.

Of the humble old functionary one may say that, if ill-regarded in life, in death he was not forgotten. With a wonderment not unalloyed with laughter the green and unknowing playgoers of a later day have been made acquainted with his sometime existence by the visitations of his shade to the place of his erstwhile activities. Of these one noteworthy instance will suffice. When Eugène Morand's and Marcel Schwob's French version of *Hamlet* was presented at the Adelphi for a spell in June 1899, with Sarah Bernhardt as the introspective Prince, a novel setting of the play scene was shown for the first time on

English boards. For the performance of the aborted tragedy a platform was erected on the prompt side, opposite to the royal dais on the O. P. In the space between sat Ophelia, with Hamlet lying by her side. At the back of the platform were flowing tapestries depicting a prospect of the castle of Elsinore, through which the players entered. Near its front were two odd-looking property trees about five feet high, symbolizing the orchard in which the action passed. Along the parapet were primitive footlights, a row of candles, which were lit by a candlesnuffer just before the play began. With all this no fault could be found. But just at the period of the murder the candlesnuffer hurriedly re-entered and with quick dispatch deftly blew out all the candles. Whoever was responsible for this arrangement, it was a grave mistake, and I can well remember the amount of laughter it, on the first night, evoked. Rigid economy of this sort, although doubtless practised in the early theatre, was certainly not a characteristic of old Court performances. Moreover, the act signified that the play had ended, which was far from being the case: there had merely been a sudden breaking off through the rising and departure of the King. Even if economy had ruled, with such a happening, the candlesnuffer would have been caught napping, and would have failed to do his duty with any alacrity. He should have come on wonderingly when all had departed, and proceeded leisurely, with many shakings of the head, to extinguish the lights.

CHAPTER XIV

SLEEPING AT THE PLAY

*E*N art, says the French proverb, *le sommeil est une opinion.* There is the weight of centuries behind that reflection: for its genesis one has to go back to Horace. It is apparently well founded; yet when one comes to apply it to sleeping at the play it is passing strange how few modern instances of its wisdom can be satisfactorily arrived at. The truth is that, although most players view them otherwise, these pleasant lapses from consciousness are generally non-committal. From Shakespeare's early day to our own playgoing has been for the most part a post-prandial pastime, and nothing is more natural for the plethoric man who has dined and wined well but to surrender himself to the deity of dreams. The merits or demerits of the play or players have nothing to do with the case. It is long since these facts were fully recognized. Recall what the Prologue said in heralding Cokayne's Caroline comedy *The Obstinate Lady*:

> And many gallants hither come, we think,
> To sleep and to digest their too much drink.
> We may please them, for we will not molest
> With drums or trumpets any of their rest.

These lines afford an excellent gloss upon what had been said apologetically a score of years previously in introducing *Henry VIII* to the Globe audience:

> 'Tis ten to one, this play can never please
> All that are here: some come to take their ease

And sleep an act or two; but these we fear
We have frighted with our trumpets.

It is remarkable that we should get no inkling of the existence of the peculiar type of playgoer here referred to in that delightfully ironic chapter in Dekker's *The Gul's Hornebooke* detailing "How a Gallant should behave in a Playhouse." Of a surety that custom must have been common enough among the gentlemen in plush to call for mock commendation. It is to be noted, however, that it was not without its attendant risks. In 1600 there fell from the press an amusing pamphlet entitled *Quips upon Questions*, by "Clonnico de Curtanio Snuffe," otherwise Robert Armin, the clown, in which one finds a rhymed quirk dealing with the folly of a roystering man about town, who, after imbibing freely, repaired to the Curtain, and there fell asleep, only to discover on coming to his senses that he had been robbed of all his money.

A humorous idea this, truly, that anybody should part with sterling coin at the playhouse door merely to indulge in sleep. With this purpose in view it would certainly be more economic and more appropriate to go in 'on the nod,' and of procedure of the sort examples are not lacking. Highly improbable as it sounds, the most notable of these graphically illustrate the possibility that a theatrical manager may deliberately woo slumber in a rival manager's theatre without intending any reflection on the quality of the fare provided there. In the days when he was controlling the destinies of Drury Lane that overworked genius of sorts Sir Augustus Harris was in the habit more often than not of procuring a much-needed 'forty winks' while seated in the stalls during Irving's memorable Lyceum first nights. With him it was never a case of being insidiously overcome. Once upon a time, as Jimmy Glover has credibly related, he deliberately took off his boots when in sole occupation of a private box at the Comedy Theatre, and, despite the fact that Charles Hawtrey was then shining there in a capital play, settled himself down to enjoy a right good nap.

For examples where sleeping at the play was in reality the expression of an opinion one has to search long and steadily before finding anything authentic. Almost as a last resource one has to fall back upon Mr Sidney Dark's agreeable book of reminiscences, *Mainly about Other People*, wherein we are told of an eminent writer who never drank anything stronger than the weakest of weak tea that

> the late William Archer exerted a more positive influence on the development of the English drama than any other contemporary critic, but his sympathies were definitely limited, and he had small patience with the merely popular. "Whenever I see Archer sleeping in the stalls on the first night," a manager once said to me, "I know I have a success."

In a free country everybody has a right to sleep, but nobody has the right to snore. Audibility is the unforgivable sin. In the course of his recollections of Bath theatricals at the close of the eighteenth century John Bernard tells us of one Captain Stanley, who, "from the rotundity of his figure and the roseate blush of his nose, bore the convivial distinction of 'the Bath Bacchus,'" that

> he was a frequent visitor to our boxes; but, however great his gratification or sympathy, he could not at all times command his senses, and would fall asleep; the result of which was that he would favour the audience with an original melody (in a pretty high key) by his nose. One evening, in the *Twelfth Night*, Orsino had repeated the lines " Sing again—oh, it comes o'er my ear like the sweet South, stealing and giving odours," when the Captain, suddenly waking,

replied with a shrill blast on his usual instrument, which disconcerted the actor and plunged the house in a convulsion of merriment.

Just here I must needs indulge in a personal reminiscence, though the story must be told somewhat at my own expense. Close on forty years ago I happened to be present at a Friday *matinée* of a comic opera at the Belfast Theatre Royal, when the whole house was much disturbed midway in the performance by the resonant snoring and gurgling of a purple-faced individual who lay back at his ease in the dress circle not far from where I sat. Ultimately, when the snorer began to enter into formidable competition with the singers for the attention of the audience, my state of irritation reached breaking-point, and I sallied forth into the lobby and made earnest appeal to the doorkeeper for the removal of the offender. Though rather startled by the request, that worthy came with me to the glass partition at the back of the circle to have the culprit pointed out, and, on this being done, said, much to my surprise, " Oh, Lord, no, sir! I daren't put that gent out. Don't you know? Why, that's Lord *X* and *Y*! "—naming the bearer of an old and honourable double-barrelled Irish title. Presumably the logic of the situation was that the man who was a real live lord had, even in the theatre, a right to be drunk as one.

But, so far as his activities in the theatre are concerned, Morpheus has never been any respecter of persons. Even absolute monarchs have yielded to his sway. It is on record that when James I was present at a performance of Gwinne's dull Latin play *Vertumnus*, during his visit to Oxford late in August 1605, he fell fast asleep. Seldom as royal lapses of the sort can be taken as such, this, one fears, was an oblique expression of opinion. When the King of Denmark visited England in 1768 he went to Covent Garden one night to see *Jane Shore*, with the blue-eyed Bellamy as Alicia, but, having fortified himself beforehand too bounteously, made no resistance to the god of sleep. To the self-centred actress this was " most tolerable and not to be endured," so—but the rest must be told in her own words:

> Unwilling that he should lose the *fine acting* it might be supposed he came to see, I drew near the box, and with a most violent exertion of voice, which the part admitted, cried out, "Oh, thou false Lord!" by which I so effectually roused His Majesty, that he told the unfortunate Comte de Bathmore (who, as I have already informed you, used to be a frequent visitor at my house) that he would not be married to a woman with such a bell voice, upon any account, as he should never expect to sleep.

When Michael Kelly, the tenor singer, in 1780, while still in his teens, sang at Florence in the opera of *Il Francese in Italia* he was honoured by the presence of the once gallant Prince Charles Edward Stuart (the uncrowned Charles III), then besotted, and marked by the ravages of grief and disappointment. We are not told precisely in Kelly's *Reminiscences* that the whilom Young Chevalier fell asleep during the performance, but the account given implies as much:

> He was at that time very old and infirm, yet there appeared the remains of a very handsome man. He was very tall, but stooped considerably, and was usually supported by two of his suite, between whom he hobbled; in this state he visited one of the theatres every night (he had a box in each); in a few minutes after he was seated he fell asleep, and continued to slumber during the whole performance. The Italians always called him the King of England, and he had the Arms

of England over the gates of his palace (the Palazzo Guadagni, in the street of San Sebastiano), and all his servants
wore the Royal Livery.[1]

Seeing that we have become a sober nation, if not
by Act of Parliament, at any rate through the rapacious
budgeting of the Chancellor of the Exchequer, there are
certain phases of theatrical history which are not likely
to repeat themselves. To-day the average new play may
have but a brief innings, but it gets a chance for its life.
Never again will there be in any abundance a type of
roystering playgoer bent on mischief, like the notorious
frequenters of the pit in Restoration days, of whom it was
said in a Drury Lane prologue of 1675 :

> One half o' the play they spend in noise and brawl,
> Sleep out the rest, then wake and damn it all.

[1] *Reminiscences* (second edition, 1826), i, 110.

CHAPTER XV

THE ROYAL BOX

FANCY pictures sometimes convey apocryphal history. To one of them is due the false impression that good Queen Bess was in the habit of going publicly to the play. Let it be said once for all that Charles II was the first English monarch to pay a visit to the theatre. Bold as was the act, it was not without French precedent, and French precedent then accounted for much. During the period of his exile the Merry Monarch acquired Gallic predilections, many of which influenced him to the end. It probably sufficed for him that Louis XIV, in the days of his adolescence, had pioneered the way. In 1656 the great success of the *Timocrate* of Thomas Corneille at the Théâtre du Marais had induced the Grand Monarch to go in state to that house. So, too, in 1659 he had repaired to the Hôtel de Bourgogne to enjoy the acting of Floridor and Mlle Beauchâteau in the *Œdipe* of Pierre Corneille. Every precaution was then taken to preserve a truly regal aloofness. As the King's box gave directly on to the *parterre*, six of his Swiss guards ranged themselves in a semicircle before him to keep the spectators at a respectful distance, and guards were also placed on the stage and at the royal entrance.

At home precedent of another and milder kind had already been set for the Merry Monarch's innovation. His gracious mother had helped to pioneer the way. More than once she had honoured the Blackfriars Theatre with her presence. On May 13, 1634, she had gone thither to see Massinger's lost play of *Cleander*; and, accompanied by the Prince Palatine, she had returned there twice early in 1636. Unhappily of these visits no gossiping letter-writer has told us anything: nothing is known of them save the bare facts.

Regarding the Merry Monarch's first visit to a public theatre, conflicting details exist. Writing long after the period from a failing memory, old John Downes, the quondam prompter, tells us in his *Roscius Anglicanus*:

> I must not forget my self, being Listed for an Actor in Sir William Davenant's Company in Lincoln's-Inn-Fields: The very first day of opening the house there, with *The Siege of Rhodes*, being to Act Haly; (the King, Duke of York, and all the Nobility in the House, and the first time the King was in a Publick Theatre). The sight of that august presence spoil'd me for an Actor too.

Downes blunders extraordinarily in his details. It is certain that his disastrous *début* on the boards cannot have taken place on the day the new theatre first opened, an event which took place late in June 1661 (the exact date is unknown); and there is therefore good reason to doubt that the day of the *début* was the day of the King's first visit. Pepys' *Diary* is useful to us in showing where Downes blundered. In it we find entered under the date Tuesday, July 2, 1661:

> Took coach and went to Sir William Davenant's Opera; this being the fourth day that it hath begun, and the first that I have seen it. To-day was acted the second part of *The Siege of Rhodes*. . . . The King being come, the scene opened; which indeed is very fine and magnificent, and well acted, all but the Eunuch, who was so much out that he was hissed off the stage.

The Eunuch was Haly, and the Haly was Downes.

Though the King was present, it is more likely to have been his second visit to the new theatre than his first. The chances are that he was present on the opening day, when the first part of *The Siege of Rhodes* was performed.

One thing, however, we do know for certain. Then was established a principle from which, in the theatre proper, there has been no deviation.[1] With us the royal box has never been wholly monopolized by royalty. The Restoration theatres had all a specific King's box, but it was only nominally the King's. So far from renting any box by the season, he paid for one only when he used it. The usual charge in Charles II's day was £10 a performance, but when opera was in the bill and the prices of admission were advanced the charge was doubled. As the King visited the theatre only by fits and starts, the result was that on afternoons when he failed to attend seats in the royal box could be obtained by anybody prepared to disburse five shillings, a slight advance on the ordinary box price; and the front row of the box came on these off-days to be the favourite haunt of the beauties of the time.

It would convey no clear idea of the relative position of the royal box in Restoration days simply to say that it occupied a central position in front of the stage and a little above stage-level, since if one is to understand the stories which are told about the happenings in and around that box one must necessarily visualize the distinguishing characteristics of the Restoration theatre. The pit then occupied the whole of the comparatively small area, but,

[1] In this respect, as in some others, the Italian Opera has ignored the English tradition. There have been few periods in the history of the King's Theatre in the Haymarket when boxes could be secured otherwise than by the season.

instead of extending under the boxes, as it does now, it ascended gradually to the base of the panel of the centre boxes. The top of the panel was no more than five feet from the pit floor at its highest point, and a person standing there in the pit could readily converse with a front occupant of the boxes. And thereby, as we shall see, there hangs a tale. But it furthermore requires to be noted that the boxes were of two kinds, distinguished as 'front' and 'side.' All the boxes had apparently four rows of benches, but the distinction was that whereas the side boxes were fully enclosed, much like the private boxes of to-day, the front boxes had only low divisions—one reason why Pepys styles them pews—and permitted their occupants to see all around.

Not until one has thoroughly grasped all these details is one in a position to comprehend Dennis's account of the beginning of Wycherley the dramatist's intrigue with the Duchess of Cleveland. " She was that night," we are told, " in the front row of the King's box in Drury Lane, and Mr Wycherley in the pit under her, where he entertained her during the whole play."

Pepys' favourite seat was somewhere near the middle of the back bench of the pit, and for very good reason. What that reason was is explained by his entry in his diary on May 1, 1667, after he had been to the Theatre Royal to see *Love in a Maze* :

> We sat at the upper bench next the boxes; and I find it pretty well, and have the advantage of seeing and hearing the great people, which may be pleasant when there is good store.

That the position, however, sometimes had for him its disadvantages is to be surmised by what he jotted down

on March 26, 1668, after being present at the first performance of *The Man is the Master*: "By and by the King
come; and we sat under him, so that I durst not turn my
back all the play." Presumably the worthy man was supposed to be hard at work in the Admiralty Office, and was
afraid of being caught neglecting his duty. One has to
bear in mind that playgoing then, as in Elizabethan days,
was an afternoon pastime. It is pretty certain that while
indulging in its more or less stolen delights he had a
divided allegiance—much to the confusion of his mind.
Only in this way can one account for the curious conclusions he came to regarding certain outstanding plays.
Often he paid much more attention to what was going
on around him than to the traffic of the scene. On the
ensuing 21st of December, after seeing *Macbeth* at the
Duke's Theatre, we find him writing:

> The King and Court there; and we sat just under them and
> my Lady Castlemayne, and close to the woman that comes
> into the pit, a kind of a loose gossip, that pretends to be like
> her, and is so, something. . . . But it vexed me to see Moll
> Davis, in the box over the King's and my Lady Castlemayne's
> head, look down upon the King, and he up to her; and so
> did my Lady Castlemayne once, to see who it was.

Macbeth was a play Pepys always much enjoyed (principally, one fears, because of the singing and dancing then
introduced into it), but on this occasion he was apparently
more concerned with the celebrities in the house than
with what was going on on the stage.

Of old in most Continental theatres the royal box was
situated in the centre of the house, and a most imposing
affair, but France soon elected to wear its rue with a
difference. In the Théâtre-Français from 1689 on for close
on a century the King's box was in the first tier on the

right-hand side immediately over the orchestra well, and the Queen's box was exactly opposite. The stage-hands, having no such convenient terms as our 'O. P.' and 'P. S.,' styled the one side of the stage *côté du roi* and the other *côté de la reine*; but after the Revolution the terms were tabooed, and the stage director of the theatre in the Tuileries substituted for them *côté cour* and *côté jardin*, in application to the Cour de Carrousel and the Jardin des Tuileries. Strange to say, notwithstanding that they had but a purely local intelligence, these terms have remained in general use in the French theatre ever since.

In our country the centrally situated royal box went out with the Stuarts. Possibly that curious factor in English life, the force of inertia, might have kept it in its pristine place had it not been for certain ruptures in Court routine. Neither the Dutchman of glorious, pious, and immortal memory nor Queen Anne ever condescended to honour the public theatre with his or her presence. Precedent was conveniently forgotten. When a royal box was once more needed it was placed laterally, close to the stage; and from that arrangement, in the theatre proper, there has been no departure. It might be thought that the change was the fruit of French example, but a reason can be found without going away from home. With the low situation of the front boxes still remaining little privacy could be obtained by renewing the old arrangement, and as the Hanoverians were not of Old Rowley's free-and-easy disposition a less approachable position for the royal box had to be selected. How close it was to the players may be gleaned from the following paragraph from a contemporary journal relative to a visit paid by George I to Rich's little theatre on March 18, 1726:

Malgramarmada, conduct of the King at Drury Lane Theatre where fired at by Hatfield

THE ATTEMPTED ASSASSINATION OF GEORGE III, MAY 15, 1800

148

Last night his Majesty went to the theatre in Lincoln's Inn Fields to see the entertainment of *Apollo and Daphne*, in which was performed a particular flying on that occasion, of a Cupid descending and presenting to his Majesty a book of the play of *The Country Wife* and the entertainment, and then ascended—at which piece of machinery the audience seemed much pleased.

But what his Majesty thought about this extraordinary method of presentation said deponent sayeth not.

From this time on until the close of the century at all theatres alike the Georges sat in the left-hand stage box. There was but one exception. At the short-lived Pantheon Opera House, which was fitted up in the prevailing Italian manner, with six tiers of secluded boxes, the royal box was placed in the centre of the first tier.

It is noteworthy that early in George II's reign certain circumstances induced the King's retinue to persuade him into visiting Covent Garden much oftener than Drury Lane. The reason was that at Drury Lane the green room was on the opposite side of the stage to the royal box, whereas at Covent Garden it was on the same side. As the gentlemen of the Court were in the habit of paying their devoirs to the actresses between the acts the more convenient access to the green room of Covent Garden made them favour that house. Then and after command nights always proved very gratifying to theatre managers, since they always brought an overflowing audience. At Drury Lane early in the last century elaborate arrangements were made on the occasions of George III's visits. The partitions in the stage box were removed, the box itself was brought forward some two feet, and a canopy of crimson velvet embroidered with gold placed over it. It was while in that box, one night in May 1800, that the King was shot at just as he had entered by a madman in the pit, much to the general consternation, although nobody was hurt.

It was long customary, on occasions when the reigning monarch visited the theatre, for him to be received at the entrance by the Lord Chamberlain, bearing lights, and to be ushered by him to the royal box. When George IV went to the King's Theatre in the Haymarket, home of Italian opera, on May 15, 1821, a curious incident happened. According to custom, he was met on his arrival by Lord Hertford, then very old and frail, who, in preceding the King upstairs, stumbled and fell. His Majesty himself at once rushed forward, and, with much solicitude, helped the veteran Chamberlain to his feet. Though much shaken, Hertford showed true grit, for he remained in the anteroom throughout the performance, and insisted on performing all the duties of his station.[1]

Something requires to be said about later times. It is interesting to note that when Edward VII visited the Covent Garden opera he much preferred using a large box on the stalls tier to the royal box immediately above it. There he was often to be seen several nights in the week, flanked by such of his intimate friends as the Marquis de Soveral and Lord Ripon. Shortly after he came to the throne George V was wont to haunt the same

[1] When the London Coliseum was first opened in 1906 a full description of the wonders of the stage and the theatre generally was given in the programme. One was told that " Through the *grand salon* is the royal entry. Immediately on entering the theatre a royal party will step into a richly furnished lounge, which, at a signal, will move softly along on a track formed in the floor, through the *salon*, and into a large *foyer*, which contains the entrance to the royal box. The lounge car remains in position at the entrance to the box, and serves as an anteroom during the performance."

box, until one night a presuming, if harmless, spectator in the stalls had the audacity in one of the intervals to lean on the edge of the box and endeavour to engage the King in conversation. It was the sort of risk Charles II ran, but somehow escaped.

CHAPTER XVI

THE GREEN ROOM

IT is natural that an individual should evince a decided partiality for one particular colour, but mysterious that the same predilection should manifest itself in a community. What occult reason ordained it that the players of yore should have pinned their faith to green? About the meridian of the eighteenth century no London theatre was reckoned complete without its green curtain, its special green boxes, its green baize carpet for its tragic heroes to die upon, or its green-coated stage attendants to come on at the end of a scene and remove the furniture. Strangely enough, however, this preponderance of the one colour affords no answer to the much-vexed question as to how the green room got its name, seeing that the name was a fortuitous afterthought. In other words, the now familiar designation and the place it indicates failed to come into existence together. History does not record when a waiting-place for the players, affording them a convenient haven of rest between their spells of activity, was first established in the playhouse. As an institution it is not to be traced before the Restoration, and when it is first spoken of it is not as the green room, but " the scene room." Pepys, in his delightful way, yields us valuable evidence upon the point. Writing in his diary on October 5, 1667, he says:

> To the King's House: and there, going in, met with Knepp, and she took us up into the tireing-rooms: and to

the women's shift, where Nell was dressing herself, and was all unready, and is pretty, prettier than I thought. And so walked all up and down the house above, and then below into the scene-room and there sat down, and she gave us fruit: and here I read the questions to Knepp, while she answered me, through all her part of *Flora's Figary's* which was acted to-day.

For the master-diarist, as for many of the gallants of his day, the scene room had perennial attractions, and it was there on a certain day in the May following that he fell a-kissing the fascinating Peg Hughes. The term was still persisting in 1678, and still implying the place where the ladies held their court, for early in that year, when Lee's *Mithridates, King of Pontus*, was produced at Drury Lane, the speaker of the epilogue was made to say:

> Faith, I'll go scour the scene-room, and engage
> Some Toy within to save the falling stage.

Though this is by no means the last we hear of the scene room, it is noteworthy that a few months later we get the first mention of the green room. In Shadwell's *A True Widow*, as brought out at the Duke's Theatre early in 1679, the scene of the early part of the fourth act is laid in the playhouse. Stanmore, later on, in referring to the fact that Selfish had forestalled him in winning the favours of Gertrude, says that " Selfish, this evening in a green room, behind the scenes, was beforehand with me." Here the phrase " behind the scenes " must be taken literally.

In the Restoration theatre, as in the theatre of Shakespeare's day, there was a tiring-house at the back of the stage, but the material difference was that, whereas in the Elizabethan era it was visible to the audience and pressed persistently into theatrical service, in the

Restoration theatre it was wholly obscured from sight. Stanmore's vague reference to "a green room" is curious, as if there were several rooms to which the term would apply; but what is still more remarkable is that for the next half-century we find the terms 'scene room' and 'green room' being used indifferently in regard to the one place.

One is accordingly prompted to hazard a guess as to how the old waiting-room got its secondary and eventually permanent designation. It sounds suspiciously like a rhyming substitution. Suppose we take it that the old scene room was usually carpeted with green baize, about the only way then in which it could have possessed a distinguishing colour? Say, an unwelcome gallant strolled in there some afternoon, and was asked quizzingly by a pert actress why he dare invade the scene room. In imagination one hears the retort, "Scene room, you call it? It looks to me more like a green room." And then, perhaps, the label stuck.

Of the subsequent contention of the rival terms for supremacy some illustrations may be given. In 1682, when, at Drury Lane, Smith spoke Dryden's epilogue signalizing the union of the two companies, he was made to say:

> We beg you last, our scene-room to forbear,
> And leave our goods and chattels to our care,
> Alas! our women are but washy toys,
> And wholly taken up in stage employs:
> Poor willing tits they are: but yet I doubt
> This double duty soon will wear them out.

A somewhat later use of the earlier term serves to drive home the fact that the time was as yet far distant when an author would be honoured with a call by way of com-

pliment on the termination of a well-received new play.
As I have already pointed out in an earlier chapter, when
Jevon spoke the epilogue to Mountfort the actor's *The
Injured Lovers* at Drury Lane in 1688 he confessed to the
jury of critics that

> My brother Mountfort in the scene-room sits,
> To hear th' censure of your sharp, quick wits.

Meanwhile the rival term was meeting with little
acceptance, but it began to gain in popularity with the
waning of the century. It crops up in *The Female Wits*,
an anonymous Drury Lane play of 1697, satirizing the
women playwrights of the time, and presenting the rehearsal of an opera. Three years later, at the same house,
Clodio in Colley Cibber's well-liked comedy *Love makes
a Man* was to be heard boasting that he knew "London
pretty well, and the side-box, Sir, and behind the scenes;
ay, and the Green Room, and all the girls and women
actresses there."

To-day, when a rehearsal is conducted in a theatre, the
players remain within hail of the producer. Things were
different a couple of centuries back. On this score I am
compelled, at the risk of boring the reader blessed with a
good memory, to quote again a passage given on an
earlier page in which Aaron Hill, writing in *The Prompter*
in 1735, makes bitter plaint of the perfunctory manner in
which rehearsing was then conducted:

> The prompter dispatches his boy [1] to the green room to
> give notice when the lady or the gentleman is waited for in
> the scene; then, in rush they, one after another, rumbling

---

[1] Almost the first specific reference to the call-boy. The actual first occurs
in *The Female Wits* (1697). According to the markings in the few extant Caroline
prompt-books, there is some reason to believe that the call-boy dates from that
period. There is no hint of him in Shakespeare's day.

their parts as they run, hurrying with a ridiculous impatience till they have catch'd and beat back the cues; and then immediately forsaking the stage, as if they had nothing to do in the play but to parrot a sound without consequence. Hence those absurd insensibilities to the passions and distresses they are acting. Hence the want of that beautiful appearance of reality which should arise from their assumed concern in what relates to themselves or others.

Remarkably enough, it was precisely at this belated date that the old name for the green room gave its last expiring flicker. There was a tragic happening in the green room of old Drury on the evening of May 10, 1735, when the as yet obscure Charles Macklin quarrelled with Thomas Hallam, his fellow-actor, over the possession of a wig, and, in the heat of passion, thrust a stick into his eye and gave him a mortal wound. At Macklin's subsequent trial for manslaughter at the Old Bailey he spoke in his own defence, and it is curious to note that both he and one of the witnesses—Thomas Arne, the father of Mrs Cibber— referred to the room where the quarrel took place as "the scene room." [1]

Meanwhile there had been some cleansing of the Augean stables. Writing in his quaint *General History of the Stage*, Chetwood, the old Drury Lane prompter of *Dunciad* memory, tells us regarding the notable trium-

[1] See the extracts from the report of the trial in Edward A. Parry's *Charles Macklin* (1891), pp. 26–27. Fifty years later Davies, writing in his *Dramatic Miscellanies* of this period, uses the term 'scene-room,' mysteriously enough, in a different sense: "There is a little open room in Drury Lane Theatre called the settle; it is separated from the stage and the scene-room by a wainscot inclosure. It was formerly, before the great green room was built, a place for many of the actors to retire to, between the acts, during the time of action and rehearsal. From time out of mind, till about the year 1740, to this place a pretty large number of the comedians used to resort constantly after dinner, which, at that time, was generally over at two o'clock. Here they talked over the news and politics of the day, though, indeed, they were no great politicians; for players are generally King's men." Of a surety this settle was the former scene room, or green room.

virate, Wilks, Booth, and Cibber, who for long controlled
the destinies of that house, that:

> For a continued course of the three managers, for more
> than twenty years, the stage was in full perfection. Their
> green rooms were free from indecencies of every kind, and
> might justly be compared to the most elegant drawing-rooms
> of the prime quality. No fops or coxcombs ever shew'd their
> monkey tricks here; but if they chanc'd to thrust in, were
> aw'd into respect. Even persons of the first rank and taste,
> of both sexes, would often mix with the performers, without
> any stain to their honour or understanding.

But the principle was bad, although it had its later
apologists. Outsiders should never have been encouraged
to go behind the scenes. The theatre is a place of work,
not play, and the obtrusion of idlers there is distracting.
In the days when there was a constant change of bill
acting demanded some concentration, but this the player
seldom got an opportunity to indulge in. All that could
possibly be pleaded in favour of the custom was advanced
in 1775 by William Cooke in his *Elements of Dramatic
Criticism*. Cooke maintained that men of rank and fashion
should be encouraged to haunt the green room, since, in
his opinion, contact with them gave the players a polish
and gentlemanly ease impossible otherwise to acquire.
Even if this were so—even if, as he implies, the gallant
Wilks of former days had gained his graces in this way—
did not the mingling bring with it as much bane as
blessing? What of the actresses? After all, were not they
the main attraction? It is pretty certain that the green
room would never have become the rendezvous of the
rakes about town if the Elizabethan custom of having
the female *rôles* acted by boys had persisted. So far as the
women of the theatre were concerned, this practice of

green-room haunting led in Restoration days to a marked debasement of the moral currency. They were spoken of as toys, and a slur was put upon the stage from which it has only just recovered.

The old London player had a stubborn pride of caste. Off the stage Hamlet did not hob-nob with Marcellus. To this reserve one finds an allusion in Fielding's *Pasquin*. During a pause in the rehearsal of his play Trapwit learns that the prompter and most of the company have retired to the green room to take tea, and he forthwith invites the First Player to accompany him there to share in the refreshment. This is awkward, because the invited one finds it necessary to reply, " Sir, I dare not go into the green room; my salary is not high enough; I shall be forfeited if I go in there." This recalls a fact apt to be forgotten—to wit, that the green room was the prerogative of the chief players, all the rest remaining in outer darkness. But for how long? The time came when a haven of rest had to be provided for the rank and file, and the problem was solved by a simple expansion of the old principle. It will be recalled that Chetwood, in the passage already cited from his book dealing with Drury Lane in the days of Wilks, Booth, and Cibber, speaks of the green rooms of that house in the plural. It would seem from this that Old Drury already possessed a second green room. The inference admits of no corroboration, but mayhap it is none the less accurate. We know that a century later the two great patent theatres had secondary green rooms. In France there was to be a still greater expansion of the principle, a circumstance which inspired the wit of Alfred Bouchard when he came, some fifty years ago, to define the term *foyer* in his bright little book *La Langue théâtrale*. This is what he says:

> **Foyer.** Salle des pas perdus où le public vient se promener dans les entr'actes. C'est un salon commun où l'on discute le mérite d'une pièce ou des acteurs, surtout au moment des débuts ou d'une première représentation.
>
> Il existe derrière le rideau un *foyer* pour les acteurs. Quand nous disons un *foyer*, comptons; car, dans cette république théâtrale, la fraternité et l'égalité existent comme . . . partout ailleurs. Nous avons donc le *foyer* des acteurs, *foyer* du chant, *foyer* des comparses. C'est donc au théâtre qu'on devrait trouver la paix, la douceur et la vertu du *foyer*. . . . Allez-y voir!

All through the eighteenth century the green room remained the happy hunting-ground of the idler. A goodly number of its frequenters were of the type of Lord Dapper in Fielding's *The Historical Register for 1736*, who, on being complimented on his powers of judgment, replied, "Not I, indeed, Mr Sourwit, but as I am one half the play in the green room talking to the actresses and the other half in the boxes talking to the women of quality, I have an opportunity of seeing something of the play, and perhaps may be as good a judge as another." Few of those who had the liberty of the green room withstood its temptations. Burly Dr Johnson seems to have been the exception. If Wilkes is to be believed he told Garrick in blunt, unquotable terms that he refrained from going thither because the white bosoms of the actresses aroused his amorous propensities. But even as the century waned the privilege of going behind at Drury Lane was eagerly sought for by the nobility. In April 1782 Richard Brinsley Sheridan wrote to the Earl of Surrey, the heir of the Dukedom of Norfolk, in reply to his request for the concession:

The Truth is that what you desire (tho' in my opinion it is a compliment from you to ask it) is a matter that does not wholly rest with me, and it is a point about which I have had some bickering with my Partners, who talk of *general rules* being broken, Partialities &c, &c.—however I hope I am settling it to your satisfaction, the Ctee. have never given any formal leave but to those who claim a right, others drop in as private friends and your L'ship will do me the honour to use that claim: and when I abandon my Power there I will do my best to leave it as a priviledge.[1]

One wonders, if the point had been put to the vote of the principal players of the time, whether the majority would have been in favour of the continuance of green-room haunting by outsiders. At least one notable actor objected seriously to the practice. Writing in his journal in 1800, George Frederick Cooke remarks:

It is very rare that a green-room conversation is worth attending to; though one might imagine from the profession of the persons who meet there, it would often be otherwise. During a representation in the evening, the strictest order and decorum ought to be preserved, particularly when it is considered how much the thoughts of those who really understand their business must be discomposed by the rude mirth and noisy talk which too often prevails there.

It was said of Burbage of old that " he was a delightful Proteus, so wholly transforming himself into his Part, and putting off himself with his Cloathes, as he never (not so much as in the Tyring-house) assum'd himself again until the Play was done." Must it not, then, be reckoned lucky for him and for those who enjoyed his art that he had not to combat the distractions of the green room? It is not surprising that most of the later players assumed their characters by fits and starts.

[1] R. Crompton Rhodes, *Harlequin Sheridan*, p. 97.

Seeing that the maintenance of Italian opera was wholly dependent on the subscriptions of the nobility and gentry, it is remarkable that the King's Theatre in the Haymarket, which had been rebuilt in 1791 after the burning down of Vanbrugh's old house, was, for over a quarter of a century, without a green room. When, in 1821, John Ebers, the bookseller, took over control of the theatre he was urged by many of the subscribers to repair the omission, and some in their eagerness offered to pay half the expense. Ebers, as he tells us in his *Seven Years of the King's Theatre*, complied with the request wholly at his own cost, but the only material advantage gained by the addition was that it afforded a place where the dancers could relax their limbs and get into proper fettle before going on the stage. But all the evidence that has come down to us goes to show that the green rooms of the early nineteenth century were conducted with the strictest propriety. A story told by Joe Cowell, the comedian, in his *Thirty Years passed among the Players in England and America* of a happening at Drury Lane in 1818 is illustrative of this:

During this season the principal green room was conducted with all the etiquette observed in an apartment designed for the same purpose in private life, and very properly too. . . . There was an obsolete forfeit of one guinea for any one entering it in undress, unless, of course, in character. This, being perfectly understood, was never likely to be incurred. But Alderman Cox, *one of the committee*, in defiance of this well-known rule, dropped in one evening in a riding dress, with very muddy boots and spurs. Tullia's train getting entangled in one of them, Oxberry goodnaturedly reminded the alderman of the forfeit, which he appeared to take (and I think did) in high dudgeon; but the next day a note was addressed to the gentlemen of the green room, begging them to accept a dozen of very fine Madeira in lieu of the guinea forfeit; pleasantly stating that, as he was a bad actor, he must be a member of the second green room, if of any, and therefore did not consider himself amenable to the laws of the first.

It was this same Alderman Cox who afterwards created a sensation by bringing an action against Edmund Kean for alienation of his wife's affections.

What Cowell conveys concerning the propriety of green-room life at Old Drury is echoed by George Vandenhoff in his *An Actor's Notebook*, while detailing particulars of his *début* at Covent Garden in 1839, when Mme Vestris ruled there. Much that he says on this score is revealing:

It must be understood that in Covent Garden and Drury Lane theatres, there was a *first* and *second* Green-Room: the first, exclusively set apart for the *corps dramatique* proper— the actors and actresses of a certain position; the second, belonging to the *corps de ballet*, the pantomimists and all engaged in that line of business—what are called the *little people*—except the principal male and female dancer, who had the privilege of the first Green-Room.

The term Green-Room arose originally from the fact of that room being carpeted in green (baize, probably), and the covering of the divans being green-*stuff*. But the first Green-Room in Covent Garden Theatre was a withdrawing room, carpeted and papered elegantly; with a handsome chandelier in the centre, several globe lights at the sides, a comfortable divan, covered in figured damask, running round the whole room, large pier and mantel-glasses on the walls, and a full-length moveable swing glass; so that on entering from the dressing room, an actor could see himself from head to foot at one view, and get back, front, and side views by reflection all round. This is the first point to attend to on entering the Green-Room, to see if one's dress is in perfect order, well put on by the dresser, hanging well, and perfectly *comme il faut*. Having satisfied him or herself on these interesting points, even to the graceful drooping of a feather, the actor or actress sits down, and enters into conversation with those around, which is interrupted every now and then by the shrill voice of the call-boy 'making his calls' (he is not allowed to enter those sacred precincts in a London theatre). . . .

The Green-Room was exceedingly comfortable during the Mathews and Vestris management. On special occasions —the opening night of the season, for example, or a ' Queen's visit '—tea and coffee were served in the Green-Room; and frequently between the acts, some of the officers of the guard, or gentlemen in attendance on the royal party, would be introduced, which led, of course, to agreeable and sometimes advantageous acquaintances.

The green room too was then the place where new plays were read to the company, and it was there that Vandenhoff heard Leigh Hunt read his *Legend of Florence* and Sheridan Knowles his *Old Maids*, the latter "in a loud, rollicking style, with marked emphasis, a theatrical effect, and strong dashes of the brogue." It is a pleasant picture he draws, but one not fated to last. The times were to change. With the downfall of the patent system came unstable managements and a decline in quality of green-room life. The handwriting was on the wall. The prime utility of the green room remained, but even that was to go. With the disruption of permanent companies in town and country in the eighties the theatre ceased to be a home and became a caravanserai. The old *camaraderie* departed. The players preferred to sit aloof in their dressing-rooms during their spells of inactivity, and the green room was converted into the star's dressing-room, or—last indignity of all—loaded up with lumber.

CHAPTER XVII

CAT-CALL DAYS

IT bodes ill for the theatre and all it stands for when the masses lose their way to it. Abstention of the sort is as ominous as the flight of rats from an unsuspected ship. In Shakespeare's day, when the drama was at its greatest, the voice of the people was the voice of God, and no other voice has since spoken with unquestioned authority. To-day, when the toiling masses are partly abandoning and partly being closed out of the theatre, there should be a warning to us of sorts in the story of Restoration times, when the theatre somehow lost its popular appeal and degenerated into a mere Court appanage. One result of this—perhaps the most appalling—was that open and honest judgment at once went by the board. The dramatist's right to a fair hearing no longer ruled. Even as early as 1663 Dryden saw fit in his prologue to *The Wild Gallant* to lament the predispositions of the lop-sided public of the time, averring that:

> Cruel factions (brib'd by interest) come
> Not to weigh merit, but to give their doom.

A decade later the deliberate damning of plays had become a regular pastime. In 1675 Shadwell, in the prologue to *The Libertine*, spoke of the so-called critics as

> Those picaroons in wit wh' infest this road,
> And snap both friend and foe that come abroad.
> This savage party crueller appears
> Than in the Channel Ostend privateers.

You, in this road, or sink or plunder all,
Remorseless as a storm on us you fall.

Otway, in a similar address written a year or two later, complained that new plays were more rudely treated than bears on the Bankside, and prayed for the exercise, at least, of Bankside law—fair play. Wycherley, in introducing *The Plain Dealer* to the Theatre Royal audience in December 1674, caustically pointed out that dog was most unnaturally eating dog, since authors were proving the greatest menace to their kind, and, though cordially hating each other, banded together to damn one another's plays. Factions of this type, he went on to say, were being aided and abetted by the noisy foplings in the pit, who, while depending upon new dramatic pabulum for their store of wit, insensately set about destroying the supply. Little, however, did he think that when he was carefully framing this very play he was actually suggesting to the malicious and the mischievous whose conduct he so execrated a new weapon of offence, or perhaps one should rather say an instrument of exquisite torture, such, indeed, as was to be applied to dramatists and players for a cool century on end. It will be recalled that in the third act of the comedy that boisterously amusing hobbledehoy Jerry Blackacre returns from a conducted tour of the booths of Westminster Hall with a variety of ear-splitting toys, on which he proceeds to give imitations of the cries of animals and the calls of birds. Among the contraptions to which he applied his lungs was a cat-call, most fatal introduction, since its shrill sounding undoubtedly suggested to the wanton-minded the most effective way in which the hopes of aspiring dramatists could be dashed.

History, in its bustling over many matters of much less

importance, has omitted to record who was the first author upon whom fell the unhappy distinction of having his work destroyed in the new way. Though it is pretty certain that the melancholy event took place not many moons after the production of *The Plain Dealer*, it is not until 1686 that one comes across any references to indulgence in cat-calling; but it is important to note that one of these references admits of the conclusion that the noxious practice had then been at least eight years in vogue. Apart from that, there is, in the first instance, potent significance in the fact that prefixed to Tom D'Urfey's *The Banditti, or A Lady's Distress*, as published in 1686, is a rambling dedication to "the extreme witty and ludicrous gent, Sir Criticall Cat-Call," since the creation of such a title implies considerable familiarity on the part of playgoers with the gent's little ways. In 1686 also there was produced at Dorset Garden Jevon the comedian's famous farce *The Devil of a Wife*, in the prologue to which, after the speaker had asked how long it was since the town had seen a new play, it was avowed that "union and cat-calls have quite spoil'd the stage"—a reference to the fact that after the amalgamation of the two companies in 1682 few new plays had been produced, and hardly any with success. More important still is it to note that Jevon, in the epistle dedicatory of his play, addressed "to my worthy friends and patrons of Locket's Ordinary," indulges in some cryptic reminiscences, which, once we conceive what he is striving to convey, fairly well approximate the period when playhouse caterwauling first began:

You may please to call to mind, and will remember that presently after our *Catcall Dissolution*, which for some time, from our natural Home and Provident Stage, dispers'd

A LUCKLESS FRENCH PLAYWRIGHT, "L'AUTEUR SIFFLÉ"

166

abroad us under-acting *Jews*, without a Moses to provide our *Manna*: and after the Players (as you may guess) of the many murmuring Hirelings, for those whose whistly breath blew 'em to a more remote and far worse climate; 'twas then the needful I (by dint of hunger forc'd) wrote (you know full well) such powerful lines to your unmindful Senate that had ye not all had Hearts of Stone, you would have melted into retaliating Favours.

The allusions here are to the discords and dissensions which occurred at the Theatre Royal in 1678, culminating in the closing of the house for a considerable time and the departure of most of the minor players for Edinburgh.

Plays of old were damned for a variety of reasons, as well as for no reason whatsoever, but perhaps the oddest way in which failure was reached was that which brought about the premature downfall of Higden's comedy *The Wary Widow*, when produced at Drury Lane in 1693. In his preface to the play the humiliated author necessarily shirked telling the whole truth, and merely pointed out that " the murmuring Israelites " and " pagans of the Pit " had completely flabbergasted the players by their " hissing, mimicking, ridiculing and cat-calling." But what really happened was that there chanced to be an excessive number of drinking scenes in the first half of the play, and, real punch having been incautiously supplied, the players soon began to feel the potent effect of their potations, with the result that they forgot their lines and made a sorry exhibition of themselves. This evoked so great a clamour that the curtain had to be let down for good at the end of the third act. And the pity of it was that *The Wary Widow* was really a good play.

Nor was it for the silencing of new plays alone that cat-calling was brought into force. Undesired revivals

were similarly burked. One of the most noteworthy
instances of this occurred at Drury Lane early in 1712
when an attempt was made to re-establish Fletcher's
comedy *The Humorous Lieutenant* in the theatrical repertory.
It was doubtless to this turning down of the thumb that
Addison referred in his delightfully whimsical essay on
cat-calling published not long after in *The Spectator*
when, after expressing his belief that the cat-call was distinctively an English device, and maintaining that its
special theatrical use was peculiar to our country, he
went on to say:

> It has at least received great improvements among us,
> whether we consider the instrument itself, or those several
> quavers and graces which are thrown into the playing of it.
> Every one might be sensible of this, who heard that remark-
> able cat-call which was placed in the centre of the pit, and
> presided over all the rest at that celebrated performance
> lately exhibited in Drury Lane.

If Addison was right in his assertion that cat-calling
was then unknown outside the English theatre we have
no option but to assume that the scandalous practice was
carried over into France at a slightly later period. A few
examples are still extant of a French colour print entitled
L'Auteur sifflé, issued in the latter half of the eighteenth
century, in which an exasperated playwright is to be seen
striding furiously across the stage after the slaughter of his
play, and tearing up his manuscript as he goes. Volleying
from six cat-calls is being directed towards him from the
parterre, and a seventh malcontent is whistling vigorously
on a door-key.

Meanwhile in England the players had stoically eaten
the leek. Cat-calling came to be looked upon by them as
inevitable, but there were sober-minded playgoers who

resented such noisy interference with their enjoyment. On this score a good story is told by Chetwood in his *General History of the Stage*. It bears reproduction:

> I remember, above twenty years past, I was one of the audience at a new play. Before me sat a sea-officer with whom I had some acquaintance; on each hand of him a couple of sparks, both prepar'd with their offensive instruments vulgarly term'd *Cat-calls*, which they were often tuning before the play began. The officer did not take any notice of them till the curtain drew up; but when they continued their sow-gelder's music (as he unpolitely call'd it), he beg'd they would not prevent his hearing the actors, tho' they might not care whether they heard or no; but they took little notice of his civil request, which he repeated again and again to no purpose. But at last one of them condescended to tell him if he did not like it, he might leave it alone. "Why, really," reply'd the sailor, "I do not like it, and would have you let your noise alone. I have paid my money to see and hear the play, and your ridiculous noise not only hinders me, but a great many other people that are here, I believe, with the same design. Now, if you prevent us, you rob us of our money and our time: therefore I intreat you, as you look like gentlemen, to behave as such." One of them seem'd mollified, and put his whistle in his pocket, but the other was incorrigible. The blunt tar made him one speech more. "Sir," said he, "I advise you once more to follow the example of this gentleman, and put up your pipe." But the piper sneer'd in his face, and clapp'd his troublesome instrument to his mouth, with cheeks swell'd out like a trumpeter to give it a redoubled and louder noise; but, like the broken crow of a cock in a fright, the squeak was stopt in the middle by a blow from the officer which he gave him with so strong a will that his child's trumpet was struck thro' his cheek and his companion led him out to a surgeon. So that we had more room and less noise, and not one that saw or heard the affair but what were well pleased with his treatment.

Powerless to remedy the evil, authors came in time to deem it politic to assume the attitude of hugging their

chains. Even Dr Johnson, indomitable as he was, could
write of himself in the prologue to *Irene* in 1749:

> Be this at least his praise; be this his pride:
> To force applause no modern arts are try'd.
> Should partial cat-calls all his hopes confound,
> He bids no trumpet quell the fatal sound.

But it was unwise to protest too much on this score,
and some authors had the misfortune to be taken at their
word. When Edward Moore's comedy *Gil Blas* was produced at Drury Lane in 1751 Garrick asked for trouble
when he provided the play with a prologue to be spoken
by Harry Woodward in the character of a critic with a
cat-call. It opened arrestingly with:

> Are you all ready? Here's your music! here! [*Blows cat-call*
> Author, sneak off, we'll tickle you, my dear.

This was so far a tempting of providence that one is not
at all surprised to find that the barometer changed at once
from 'set fair,' and that the play had difficulty in weather-
ing the storm.

A score of years passed without bringing any serious
betterment of the conditions. Authors continued to joke
over their servility. Said the prologue to Kelly's *A Word
to the Wise*, when that ill-fated comedy was brought out
at Old Drury in 1770:

> A roasted poet is a glorious meal—
> And oft I've known a miserable wit,
> Through downright laughter fasten'd on the spit,
> Basted with cat-call sauce for very fun,
> Not till quite ready—but still quite undone.

About the last time a cat-call was ever heard in an
English theatre was at Covent Garden late in 1809 during
the prolonged O. P. riots. Perhaps the main reason why

AN INCIDENT DURING THE O.P. RIOTS AT COVENT GARDEN

From a coloured print of the time: "Acting magistrates committing themselves, being their first appearance on this stage, as performed at the National Theatre, Covent Garden, September 18, 1809."

170

it then fell into desuetude was that it proved a very mild weapon of offence compared with most of those the determined opponents of advanced prices brought into play. We read that night after night watchmen's rattles, dustmen's bells, and French horns and bugles were regularly resorted to with the aim of preventing the performance from being heard. It is even said that now and again a party of three or four pleasant fellows brought live pigs into the pit, and when a lull came in the storm stirred things up by pinching them vigorously. Well, well, what dull and decorous dogs we have since become!

CHAPTER XVIII

FOPS' CORNER

PLAIN facts are sometimes difficult to reconcile. When one comes to think of it it is astonishing to the verge of incredibility to find that the century which began with Shakespeare and ended with Congreve, or, in other words, gave us all that is greatest in our drama, should have been precisely the century when concentration in the theatre was most difficult and least practised. Many generations passed before the English (or, indeed, any) audience could discipline itself for the common good. How fine thoughts finely expressed could have been properly savoured amid intermittent hurly-burly is incomprehensible, unless we are prepared to assume that our forebears were devoid of nervous sensibility and capable of ignoring distractions. Insensitive they certainly were not : their emotions lay on the surface. It was exactly because the natural man was given free play that noise abounded.

Given a standing pit, and, let the country be what it may, you are bound to have a restive audience. To the theatrical antiquary who looks far afield that has long been a truism. In the common playhouses of what is broadly known as the Elizabethan period the groundlings, jostling one another in the open yard, were seldom in a stage of perfect quietude. A Jacobean writer, describing the aspect from above, dwells upon the perpetual motion :

> The very floor, as 'twere, waves to and fro,
> And, like a floating island, seems to move
> Upon a sea bound in with shores above.

It might have been thought that with the banishment of the groundling at the Restoration peace would have reigned in the theatre, but, so far from the seating of the pit bringing any amelioration, for the one devil that was then cast out nearly seven rushed in to fill the vacancy. The Restoration theatre was a theatre of the classes rather than the masses, but its public lost no time in demonstrating that riot and disorder were not the proud prerogative of the great unwashed. Between the drunken gallants of the time brawls in the pit were of common occurrence: there was much flashing of swords and considerable screaming from the frightened ladies above in the boxes. Nor was this the worst. There was no booking of seats in those days, and very shortly it grew to be customary for those who desired good places to send their servants early to the theatre and secure them by sheer bodily possession. Once the real owners arrived the flunkeys betook themselves to the vestibule, and there remained until the time came to escort their lords and ladies home. Meanwhile they indulged in their own amusement, often quarrelling among themselves like their betters, and usually contrived to create a racket the noise of which rang with painful clarity through the theatre. It was of these liveried gentry that Dryden wrote in an epilogue delivered in 1682:

> They've grown a nuisance, beyond all masters,
> We've none so great—but their unpaying masters.

(There is a side-slap here at the gallants who came to the play on tick, or, worse still, sought to evade payment by dodging the boxkeeper.)

As if all this were not bad enough, the witlings of the time inconsiderately contributed their material quota to the general disturbance. Fops' Corner, both the institution and its label, was completely symbolic of the temper of the times. It signified a particular angle of the pit close to the stage (but whether on the right or the left we know not), where the *beaux* were accustomed to assemble and act a silly farce of their own improvising. One must needs recall that the orchestra well in those days did not extend, as now, along the whole width of the stage, having fewer musicians to accommodate, and that standing room was left on either side. This arrangement held good until the dawn of the last century. In vain did the dramatists of the hour rail in good, round, set terms against the play within the play so distractingly presented by the witlings of the corner. Nothing short of a special visitation of providence could have annihilated this disgraceful institution, though circumstances now and again conspired to bring about a temporary cessation of the nuisance. When Dryden's *Marriage à la Mode* was produced at the Duke's Theatre in the Easter of 1672 the epilogue gave thanks for small mercies in commenting on the fact that most of the rakes about town had betaken themselves on shipboard to fight against the Dutch:

> Lord, how reform'd and quiet are we grown!
> Since all our braves and all our wits are gone.
> Fop Corner now is free from civil war,
> White Wig and Vizard masks no longer jar.
> France and the Fleet hath swept the Town so clear,
> That we can act in peace, and you can hear.

But the quietude gained by sheer loss of patrons was by no means desirable, since heads counted even when they were empty, and it was with an odd sigh of relief that the players welcomed back the old disturbers. Even Dryden came in time to accept the inevitable. His epilogue, written to be spoken at new Drury Lane on its

THE FITZGIGGO RIOT AT COVENT GARDEN IN 1763
From the Gabrielle Enthoven Collection, Victoria and Albert Museum, London.

opening day in March 1674, concludes resignedly with

> So may Fop Corner full of noise remain,
> And drive far off the dull attentive train.

Not that the fop always remained in his corner. Occasionally he grew restless and flitted about the house. Four years later we find Goodvile, in Otway's comedy *Friendship in Fashion*, promising an aspiring woman of the town that she shall keep her coach and six,

> and every morning swoop the Exchange in triumph, and after noon in the theatre, exalted in a box, give audience to e'ry trim, amorous, twirling fop of the Corner that comes thither to make a noise, hear no play, and show himself.

By this time it had become a favourite pastime of the Restoration poet to bait the foplings. Seeing that they vexed the staider members of the audience quite as much as they vexed the players, and were, moreover, hopelessly in the minority, they formed a safe mark. Thus we find Shadwell in his epilogue to Maidwell's *The Loving Enemies* in 1680, after complaining that the theatre's old patrons were busying themselves in perusing libellous pamphlets, instead of continuing to go to the play, admitting that there were some exceptions, although such as the players could do well without:

> In none of these will the young sparks delight,
> They never read, and scorn all those who write.
> They only come the Boxes to survey,
> Laugh, roar and bawl, but never hear the Play.
> In monkey tricks they pass the time away,
> At least, the Poet hopes th've done to-day.

Afterwards, seeing that there must always be some proportion of drones in the human hive, Fops' Corner came to be looked upon as a necessary evil, the sort of thing sensible people comment upon with a shrug of the shoulders, and reference to it ceases. About the last mention of the unsavoury meeting-place to be found before the end of the century occurs in Radcliffe's " anti-heroick poem " of *The Ramble*, published in 1682:

> Then it began to visit plays,
> And on the women it would gaze,
> And looked like Love in a Maze
> Or a wood.
> Into Fop Corner it would get,
> And use a strange obstreperous wit,
> Nor any quiet to the Pit
> Allowing.

Once a foolish custom is allowed to take root goodness only knows how long it will persist! The mere force of inertia keeps it alive. Viewed as a matter of course and with silent contempt, the old asinine playhouse practice lingered so long that it is impossible to say when it ended. All we know for certain is that it had an existence of something over half a century. Our last trace of it is in a pleasant essay on "Audiences " in a small book of diversified pleasings called *The Touchstone*, written by James Ralph, of *Dunciad* memory, and published in 1728. Therein, strangely enough, it is given brevet honours and inaptly styled Wits' Corner.

CHAPTER XIX

AFTER-MONEY

STAGE history has never been made, and should not be written, in watertight compartments. The law of the theatre, as of life, is continuity amid change. Yet when one comes to trace the origin of that widespread mid-nineteenth century rule " Half-price at nine o'clock " [1] it becomes clearly apparent the deeper one delves that effects cannot always be taken to have a logical association with their primary causes. The whole truth on this point has been tardy in arriving, owing to missing links in the chain of evidence; and it is only by a careful marshalling of all the facts—some of which have only just been discovered—that one is able to demonstrate that the first taking of a second price at the play arose from a question of privilege created by a desire on the part of the public to prolong a remarkable Elizabethan custom.

With us no principle has been more consistently maintained or more sturdily fought for than established right of way, and the question in case was one of that order. It needs to recall that in the open theatres of the early seventeenth century admission-money was paid direct to the doorkeepers (otherwise known as 'gatherers'), and that after the play had got well under way—say, at the end of the third act—the doorkeepers forsook their posts and carried their money-boxes to the treasurer's room in

[1] See T. F. D. C[roker]. on " Half-price," in *The Era Almanack* for 1878, p. 57. The system died out in London in the early seventies, but it lasted in the provinces somewhat longer.

the tiring-house. This procedure was necessitated by the fact that the principal players shared the receipts with the house-owners after the daily expenses had been deducted, and that the dividends were made up and paid over without delay. There was little need for the gatherers to return to their posts once they had discharged their responsibilities, no straggler being foolish enough to pay good money for less than half a play, and it was customary for them to remain behind and take humble part in the traffic of the scene as supers.

With these facts in mind it is easy to understand that in process of time there sprang up a lax custom of allowing free admission once the performance was half over, and how what in the beginning was an unpremeditated concession came eventually to be considered an inalienable right. But what is remarkable about the matter is that, so far from writing *finis* to the old privilege, the Civil War and the Commonwealth merely brought about a temporary disagreeable interruption. When the King came to his own again those who had previously been playgoers resumed their old habits just as if nothing of more than transient importance had happened. Vainly did the newly appointed patentees strive to create a wholly new order of things in the new type of theatre they had established. In response to their plaints Charles II issued printed proclamations from time to time with the view of regulating the methods of playgoing, but not on all points with complete success. Five times between 1663 and 1674 is he to be found fulminating against sundry abuses, including the playgoers' " pretended privilege by custom of forcing their entrance at the fourth or fifth acts without payment," but, so far as any improvement took place on this score, his thunderbolts proved squibs. It suited the Restoration gallant to constitute the playhouse a place of regular rendezvous, apart from its office as a place of theatrical entertainment; and, although backed up half-heartedly by the King, the patentees never summoned up fortitude enough to act upon their powers.

Right of way or no right of way, it is obvious that laxities of this order could not last for ever, and a change came over the spirit of the playgoer's dream. In 1682, by an extraordinary arrangement, there was brought about a union of the two companies, whereby each of the two theatres was to be occupied alternately in an economic way by the one set of players. Monopoly then was able to correct abuses that rivalry had to some extent fostered. The public were no longer masters of the situation. In 1686 Alexander Davenant, one of the capitalists of the combine—an insinuating rogue who brought infinite discredit to the honoured name he bore—suggested to his associates, with a well-assumed disinterestedness which masked his ulterior aim, that some attempt should be made to increase the receipts by extracting a little money out of the pockets of the late-comers who had been so long allowed to walk in free. The impost was not to be so serious as to arouse violent opposition, nothing more than sixpence to the half-crown pit or a shilling to the four-shilling boxes. The experiment was at once tried, and, strange to say, the principle of 'after-money,' as it was long called, was forthwith established without creating any particular trouble. For several seasons the proceeds of this second price were given as a bonus to the players, who thereby gained between £400 and £500 a year. Then the wily and oily Alexander began to show his hand.

In 1692, he obtained an order from the Court of Chancery authorizing him to farm out the after-money for sixteen years at a fine of £1000, £800 of which was to go to pay off a debt owing by the theatres, and the balance to form a modest reserve fund. The fine, in the circumstances, was so inadequate that it is not surprising to learn that Davenant's real intention was to assign the lease to some person in trust for himself. For a time he triumphed; but in a little over a year his manifold duplicities and embezzlements came to light, and he fled the country.[1]

The main result of Davenant's machinations was that disputes began between the capitalists of the combine and the players which culminated in rupture. The question of the allocation of the after-money became a bone of contention, and was prominent among the factors that decided Betterton and his train in 1695 to leave the fold and set up a third theatre. Nor was this the only way in which Davenant's scheming proved instrumental in bringing about important changes in theatrical affairs. Almost from its very institution the principle of after-money had a potent, and by no means beneficial, influence on the trend of dramaturgy. There is a world of difference between the mental attitude of the spectator who gets admission free in the middle of the performance, purely on sufferance, and the mental attitude of the spectator who pays whatever sum may be demanded, let it be never so small. In the one case there could be no examination of the gift horse in the mouth; in the other something of substantive interest had to be given for money taken, and it could not be yielded by the last act or so of an ordinary five-act play. Moreover, it was seen that to solve the

[1] Leslie Hotson, *The Commonwealth and Restoration Stage*, pp. 289–293.

problem would be to win the support of a section of
the public that had not for years frequented the theatre—
that very considerable mercantile and shopkeeping class
which found itself unable to get to the theatre betimes.
At first the sprats thrown out to catch these particular
mackerels were very small sprats indeed. We learn of
them in the prologue to Sedley's *Bellamira*, as delivered
in 1687:

> Now you come hither but to make your Court:
> Or from adjacent Coffee houses throng
> At our fourth act for a new Dance or Song.

But the new type of belated playgoer was not to have
his yearning stomach stayed by snacks, and soon it was
found that incidental excrescences of this order, though
pleasing enough in their way, were too trifling to suffice.
The difficulty was to know how to introduce any sort of
material substantive entertainment into the last act or so
of a play; but at the expense of relevancy and shapeliness
the post-Restoration playwrights solved it. Terminal
masques of a more or less elaborate order were for a time
exceedingly popular. Of this convention the curious will
find examples in *Dioclesian, or The Prophetess* (1690), *The
Indian Queen* (as revived in 1695), *The Anatomist* (1696), and
The Island Princess (1699). It is noteworthy, furthermore,
that in the period represented by these plays spectacular
opera (or perhaps one should rather say operatic spectacle)
was much to the fore—a fact not without its significance
in this connexion, seeing that at practically any juncture
throughout elaborately mounted musical drama generally
presents something to gratify both eye and ear. Near the
end of the century the influence of the unsophisticated
playgoer is also to be traced in the giving between the

acts of what would now be styled variety turns, acrobatic feats, dancing, and what not.

But for a somewhat cryptic allusion in an early eighteenth-century prologue we should have no clue to the relative scale of prices charged during the second period of admission, and conversely, but for the recent discovery of the establishment of the principle of after-money, we should not be able to understand the allusion. As a matter of fact, it has been misinterpreted.[1] In the prologue to D'Urfey's comedy of *The Bath*, as spoken at Drury Lane in 1701, we read:

> I'm told that Beaux with Perukes cover'd o'er,
> Make such strange shifts to save poor shillings four;
> They'll in Side-Box three Acts for nothing sit,
> At last sneak down for Six-pence to the Pit.

Admission-money then and earlier to the boxes was not paid at the door on entering, but to the boxkeeper, who went his rounds between the acts. The reference here is to a trick of box-haunting *beaux* of an impecunious order, who contrived by shifting about to see three acts for nothing, and then, when the period of after-money had been reached, got into the pit for sixpence. Apparently from the first introduction of the principle of after-money admission at the reduced rates was allowed at the end of the third act, not, it is to be noted, as at a much later period, at a particular hour. The later arrangement was much more convenient.

The taking of a modest second price had a large measure of appeal for others besides the shopkeeper and the clerk. For economic reasons it proved very grateful to members of the oldest known profession. In the

[1] Allardyce Nicoll, *Restoration Drama*, p. 14.

'best-seller' of its day, *The London Spy* of 1700, Ned Ward indulges in a quaint revealing simile in relating of Gray's Inn Walks how certain ladies "began to flow into the Walks, as whores into the eighteen-penny Gallery at the third Act." Evidently he meant at the end of the third act. As eighteenpence was then the full price of the middle gallery the second price there, on the basis of sixpence to the half-crown pit, must have been a mere trifle.

Apart from bringing the masses back to the playhouse, whither they had lost their way in Restoration days, the most vital change brought about by the institution of a second price was the firm establishment of the afterpiece. Of extreme benefit, if only because it was the means of releasing our dramatists from the tyranny of the five-act form, this alteration of routine dated from the second decade of the eighteenth century. It is true that from 1676 (when Otway appended *The Cheats of Scapin* to his adapted Duke's Theatre tragedy *Titus and Berenice*, because it was written in three short acts) terminal farces had been occasionally produced before that period, but not of such frequency as to indicate a dawning custom. It would appear that the actual initiator of the new system was Aaron Hill, who, when his tragedy of *Elfrid, or The Fair Inconstant*, was produced at Drury Lane on January 9, 1709/10, tacked on to it an amusing new farce of his own called *The Walking Statue, or The Devil in the Wine Cellar*. It cannot be but that this whimsical trifle met with considerable success (it certainly lived much longer than the tragedy), for, following it, there came an eruption of similar afterpieces. Emulating Hill's example, Charles Johnson had two plays of his produced at the Queen's

Theatre in the Haymarket on April 20 ensuing—a tragedy called *The Force of Friendship* and a farce called *Love in a Chest*. At the same house in June was brought out Colley Cibber's burlesque *The Rival Queans, with the Humours of Alexander the Great*; and at Drury Lane in the following year the same author's long-popular *Hob, or The Country Wake*. Of the vogue of afterpieces at this particular period we get full indication in Johnson's preface to *The Force of Friendship*, when he came, shortly after their production, to publish his allied tragedy and farce together:

> If this can be any proof of the Licentiousness of the Age we live in, it may be urg'd with some force, when we see no audience can bear the fatigue of two hours' good sense tho' Shakespeare and Otway endeavour to keep 'em awake, without the promis'd relief of the *Stage Coach*,[1] or some such solid afterlude: a few lines, indeed, are now and then forced down their throats by the help of this gewgaw, 'tis tack'd to the tragedy or the Tragedy to that, for 'tis the Money Bill; the actors may design it as a dessert, but they generally find the palates of their guests so vitiated that they make a meal of whipped cream, and neglect the more substantial food which was design'd for their nourishment.

Much later on a clear echo of this stricture was to come in *The Vicar of Wakefield*, where the Strolling Player informs Dr Primrose with due irony that Fletcher, Ben Jonson, and the works of Shakespeare are "the only things that go down," and when the Doctor, mistaking his tone and putting a literal interpretation on his words, gives vent to his astonishment the player adds, by way of explanation, that the public "only go to be amused, and find themselves happy when they can enjoy a pantomime

---

[1] Farquhar and Motteux's farce *The Stage Coach* was first printed in Dublin in 1704, but had apparently been acted in London in 1701.

under the sanction of Jonson's or Shakespeare's name."
As this remark has been taken to mean that Shakespeare
had been vitiated by pantomimic interpolations [1] it is as
well to point out that during the greater part of the
eighteenth century the performance of pantomimes was
not confined to any particular season, and that entertainments of the sort were generally given as afterpieces to
weightier fare.

With the care taken in catering for the second-price
public and the steady increase in its numbers there came
a gradual advance in the charges. By 1732 the late-comer
could no longer get admission to the pit for sixpence. A
prologue spoken at Drury Lane in that year on the
occasion of the revival of Fielding's *The Author's Farce*
testifies to the preponderance of the second-price public
in making plaint that:

> No longer now we see our crowded door
> Send the late-comer back again at four.
> At seven now into our empty pit
> Drops from his counter some old prudent cit,
> Contented with twelve pennyworth of wit.

In those days the doors opened at five, the performance
began at six, and the full price to the pit was, as of yore,
half a crown. There is here a longing for the return of the
good old times, when the house filled as soon as the doors
were opened. A crowded house at the end did not compensate for a half-empty house at the beginning. The
staid playgoer who desired to take his amusement in peace
might very well have said "Amen" to this plaint, for the
taking of after-money had for him certain disadvantages.
Writing in *The Connoisseur* in 1754 on "Audiences," an

---

[1] See David Nichol Smith, *Shakespeare in the Eighteenth Century*, pp. 18–19.

anonymous essayist takes occasion to rebuke the late-comers for their turbulence, and earnestly recommends

> the gentlemen who draw the pen from under their right ears about seven o'clock, clap on a bag-wig and sword, and drop into the boxes at the end of the third act, to take their half-crown's worth with as much decency as possible; as well as the bloods who reel from the taverns about Covent Garden near that time, and tumble drunk into the boxes.

The term 'after-money' lingered long in theatrical parlance. It was still in use at Covent Garden in 1772, when separate accounts continued to be kept of the first and second takings.

CHAPTER XX

'GOLD TICKETS'

NOTHING is more indicative of the vast changes
made in theatrical routine within the past century
than the disuse among players of certain old phrases with
which all theatrical folk were once familiar, but whose
significance is now lost to everybody save the burrowing
antiquary. Time was when the magic words 'gold tickets'
conjured up rosy visions to the needy actor, but so far
have ways and means altered that they have long ceased
to form a delightful abracadabra. Viewed, however, from
the present-day pinnacle of sturdy independence, the term
connotes servitude and humiliation, for, not to put too
fine a point upon it, the 'gold ticket' of old was nothing
better than a gratuity. A custom rather than a principle,
and even as a custom not to be reckoned upon, it was
a contingency of the annual benefit in the old stock-
company days, when the player was engaged by the season
or for a term of years.

Although dramatists had been given benefits from
Shakespeare's time (generally on the third day of a new
play), the principle of the benefit was not extended to the
player until the Restoration, and then only partially. Next
to the authors the actresses were the first benefit-takers,
and with them initially the benefit was a joint affair.
Writing in his *Diary* on September 28, 1668, Pepys records
how a messenger called on him with the information
" that the women's day at the playhouse is to-day, and

that therefore I must be there, to encrease their profit."
So off he hastened to the Theatre Royal, where *The City
Match* was to be revived for the occasion, and there found
himself one of a large audience, including the King and
his Court. Subsequently well-nigh a score of years passed
before any player was accorded an individual benefit.
That distinction fell upon Mrs Barry, the first Queen of
Tragedy, and for some few years from 1687 on it remained
her annual prerogative. As her salary, despite her emi-
nence, never exceeded 50s. a week the concession doubtless proved a grateful supplement to her income.

How the principle of the annual benefit came to be
diffused and to grow into a recognized institution has been
told by Colley Cibber in his *Apology*. A serious situation
arose in 1695, when Betterton opened the new theatre in
Lincoln's Inn Fields and the players of Drury Lane found
themselves deserted. So depleted became their exchequer
that the patentees of the old house could do no better than
pay the players half in specious promises and half in ready
money. Cibber goes on to say:

> In this precarious condition some particular actors (how-
> ever binding their agreements might be) were too poor or
> too wise to go to law with a lawyer, and therefore rather
> chose to compound their arrears for their being admitted to
> the chance of having them made up by the profits of a benefit
> play. This expedient had this consequence—that the paten-
> tees, though their daily audiences might, and did, some-
> times mend, still kept the short subsistence of their actors
> at a stand, and grew more steady in their resolution so to
> keep them, as they found them less apt to mutiny while their
> hopes of being cleared off by a benefit were depending. In
> a year or two these benefits grew so advantageous that they
> became at last the chief article in every actor's agreement.

Little did the players of Old Drury imagine that when

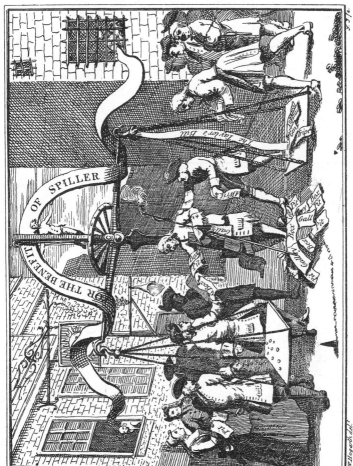

HOGARTH'S TICKET FOR SPILLER'S BENEFIT, 1728

they fought for the establishment of the annual benefit they were making rods for the backs of generations of players to come, and laying up for them a store of humiliation. But that is the way of the world. We never do anything for posterity, because posterity has done nothing for us. Though the profits of a benefit night were rarely, if ever, assured, seeing that the daily charges of the house (anything from £40 upward) had to be paid for out of the takings, the managers took advantage of the swallowing of the bait to cheapen the market. It is true that some of the great players of the mid-eighteenth century, such as Spranger Barry and Peg Woffington, had excellent salaries, but the rank and file hardly had a living wage. To ensure the success of his benefit the actor had to put his pride in his pocket, and, equipped with a bundle of tickets and a sheaf of playbills, wait obsequiously upon the nobility and gentry in the hope of making sales. Rebuffs were not frequent when the applicants were players of any consequence; on the contrary, it became customary among fashionable people, when taking tickets, always to pay for them in gold. Even if only a couple of four-shilling box tickets were purchased a guinea would be tendered in exchange. Hence the principle of 'gold tickets.'

One digresses here momentarily to point out that William Cooke, when writing on *The Elements of Dramatic Criticism* in 1775, correctly dates the inception of the benefit system from the dawn of the century, and holds forth on its banefulness. It had led to the scaling down of the minor salaries, with the result that the rank and file were forced to haunt the taverns to pick up acquaintances with the view of making a good benefit, instead of devoting their leisure to the study of their art. Intimacy with a wide circle of playgoers became essential, and the consequent dissipation and extravagance generally culminated in disaster. Thus it was that the very subsistence of the minor fry depended on being right, good, rollicking fellows, rather than on their capacity as players.

Old theatrical customs can seldom be traced to their source, but as it happens we know exactly how the principle of 'gold tickets' sprang into being. It was not through any pitiful plaint from an ill-paid minor player, though it was precisely this class that had most claim to the bounty. On the contrary, it was in connexion with the benefits of the three greatest players of the end of the seventeenth century that the custom had its origin. This would be in 1696 or thereabouts. In 1705 one finds the anonymous author of *The Lunatick* rejoicing in his caustic dedication over the downfall of the little Lincoln's Inn Fields Theatre, and pouring vitriol into the wounds of its managers. He tells Betterton, Mrs Barry, and Mrs Bracegirdle that now the times are changed there can be "no more taking benefits in the best season of the year, and dunning quality for guinea tickets." But if he reckoned that the principle of the 'gold ticket' was about to lapse he made a huge mistake. Betterton himself was soon to show him otherwise. When the veteran actor announced his benefit at Drury Lane in April 1709 all the world and his wife, under the impression that he was about to take his farewell of the stage, rushed to procure tickets at any price, with the result that, irrespective of the house-money, his receipts from 'gold tickets' alone, if Steele is to be believed, amounted to at least £450.[1]

[1] Robert W. Lowe, *Thomas Betterton*, pp. 178–180.

Curiously enough, though the system of the annual benefit was adopted in the Dublin theatre very shortly after it was instituted in London, the allied custom of 'gold tickets' had no recognition in the Irish capital until the middle of the eighteenth century, or about forty years later.[1] Considering that the old Irish nobility and gentry were prodigal to a fault, this delay is puzzling to account for. When the practice was discountenanced for so long it is difficult to know how it ever got a footing. If it was a pure matter of dignity and self-respect on the part of the Irish player, how came it that that commendable attitude was allowed to lapse? Perhaps its upspringing was due to the occasional visits of London stars, who naturally looked on their benefit nights for these *douceurs*, and were not above giving a hint to that effect. Whatever the reason, the early abstention from the custom had one remarkable result. Since, in the conditions, no very bounteous return was to be looked for from a benefit, the Dublin player of the first half of the century held out for a better stipend than was usually paid to one of his rank across the water, and generally got it. A bird in the hand being much more satisfactory than two in the bush, it is not at all surprising that the minor Irish player stuck like a limpet to his job, and seldom had thoughts of adventuring across the channel. Not a few of them spent their whole life in the gay little Irish capital.

The derogatory system of the 'gold ticket' lasted long, but not so long as the benefit system with which it was allied. Boaden records that when Mrs Siddons took her

[1] Tate Wilkinson records in his *Memoirs* that when he took his benefit at Smock Alley in 1758 the receipts of the house were £154, without reckoning "gold tickets to a considerable amount, not only from my friends and some persons of distinction, but particularly from the gentlemen of the army."

second benefit at Drury Lane in March 1783 the receipts were "no less a sum than £650," but he is careful to add that "Lady Spencer gave 90 guineas for her side box, and Lady Aylesbury a bank-note of £50 for an upper box," and there were doubtless other benefactions of the sort. Surprising, however, as the sum seemed to him, it had long been excelled on an occasion of the sort. It is not all gospel that George Anne Bellamy preaches in her *Apology*, but it may nevertheless be true, as she states, that her benefit at Covent Garden in 1756 made her £1100 the richer, since she is good enough to explain that Lord Kildare, Lord Granby, Mr Fox, and Mr Digby paid £100 each for their tickets.

Once in a while a 'gold ticket' was the herald of prolonged good fortune to a deserving actress. When Harriet Mellon announced her benefit at Cheltenham in September 1805 most of the visitors to the spa were importuned to take tickets, Thomas Coutts, the immensely rich and remarkably eccentric old banker, among the number. Coutts sent her five glittering guineas fresh from the Mint, together with a polite note begging that a box be kept for him, and expressing the hope that the enclosure would prove "luck-money." Superstitious to a fault, Harriet for long treasured the coins as such, and so, indeed, they proved. Had that 'gold ticket' never been proffered it is pretty certain she would never have become the richest woman of her time, or donned in real life a duchess's coronet. How all that came about is now a twice-told tale, but those who have never heard it— there are people who still ask, "What are Keats?"—may be commended to its neat telling in Fyvie's *Comedy Queens of the Georgian Era*.

THE
AUTHORS
BENEFIT
PASQUIN

Theatrical
Barometer

Comm
Sense
Trag
Com

Folly

At y̆ Theatre in y̆ Hay-market

FIELDING'S BENEFIT TICKET AT THE HAYMARKET, 1736

192

Generation after generation passed, and no sign came of the player's awakening to a sense of his degradation. It was not a matter of the jingle of the guinea salving the wound that honour felt, for the old histrionic conscience had no Achilles' heel. When Edmund Kean, after his great triumph at Drury Lane in 1814, announced his first benefit there at the end of the season an unceasing flow of fashionable folk set in towards his house. A gentleman who called upon him, ostensibly to buy a ticket, but largely to gratify his curiosity, found to his amazement that money was scattered carelessly all about the room. Piles of bank-notes were to be seen on the mantelpiece, and Kean's child was rolling about on the floor playing with abundant guineas.

Happily, however, only a few years were to elapse before that *rara avis*, a high-principled actor of prominence, was to make a resolute stand against the old degrading practice. It was Kean's successor, Macready, who drove the nails into its coffin. When he was the leading, and highly popular, tragedian at Covent Garden in 1820 he refused, on taking his benefit there in June, to accept more for his tickets than their legitimate price, avowing that the old system of largesse flagrantly compromised the actor's independence. Although his repeated rebukes in this way to the profession he adorned ultimately served their purpose, still one must recall, as the cynic said, that to be virtuous is to be eccentric, a potent reason why a good many moons were to pass before Macready's eccentricity became normality.

CHAPTER XXI

SINGING AUDIENCES

BECAUSE of its basic impulsiveness and inflammability there is nothing in life more paradoxical than the Gallic temperament. Logically minded as they undoubtedly are, the French are capable of rank illogicality; and although their inherent taste and refinement have long since established them as paragons they can descend with alacrity into the ring and clown it with a whole-souled *abandon*. One recalls in this connexion a curious habit of the old French opera-goer, especially as it is a peculiarity that French sociologists and musical historians have for the most part elected to ignore.[1] The truth of the story is so far stranger than fiction that it would be unbelievable on a mere *ipse dixit*, but, happily, chapter and verse can readily be given in confirmation of its accuracy. Let me in the first place put Addison into the witness-box. In the course of some general reflections on opera in the twenty-ninth number of *The Spectator* he writes:

> The Musick of the French is indeed very properly adapted to their pronunciation and accent, as their whole opera wonderfully favours the genius of such a gay, airy people. The chorus in which that opera abounds gives the *parterre* frequent opportunities of joining in consort with the stage. This inclination of the audience to sing along with the actor so prevails with them, that I have sometimes known the performer on the stage do no more in a celebrated song

[1] The exception is V. Fournel, who, in his *Curiosités théâtrales* (1878), p. 201, makes reference to the old custom, and cites from Addison on the point.

than the clerk of a parish church, who serves only to raise the Psalm, and is afterwards drown'd in the musick of the congregation.

Thus, spontaneous and deep-down, were the beginnings of community singing. It will not be difficult to show that no spice of humorous exaggeration flavours Addison's account, and that, so far from the matter discussed being a transient affair, the whim and folly of an hour, it was then a confirmed habit. Exactly a quarter of a century previously (or, to speak by the card, in 1685) Dryden, in his prologue to the opera of *Albion and Albanius*, had commented upon the Parisian practice, and in such a way as to convey to us that nothing of the sort had been attempted in England:

> In France the oldest man is always young,
> Sees operas daily, learns the tunes so long,
> Till foot, hand, head, keep time with every song.
> Each sings his part, echoing from pit to box,
> With his hoarse voice, half harmony, half pox;
> "Le plus grand roi du monde" is always ringing,
> They show themselves good subjects by their singing.
> On that condition set up every throat,
> You Whigs may sing for you have chang'd your note.
> Cits and Cittesses, raise a joyful strain,
> 'Tis a good omen to begin a reign:
> Voices may help your charter to restoring,
> And get by singing what you lost by roaring.

Evidently Grabut's leaden score was not tunable enough to induce either Whig or Cit to raise their voices in response to this appeal, and, the good omen being lacking, the reign of James II had no choice but to end badly. The post-Restoration gallant already possessed a full budget of playgoing improprieties, and had no desire to add to the number.

A good story is told of Matthew Prior's experience at

the French *opéra*. He was seated beside a gentleman who persisted in raising his voice in unison with one of the principal male vocalists every time he sang. At last irritated beyond endurance, he proceeded to hiss and boo the stage performer. Astonished at this, his tormentor asked him what reason he had for his strident disapproval. " Every reason in the world, my good sir," replied Prior. " The fellow makes so much noise that I actually cannot hear you sing."

At a slightly later period Gay had a similar experience but, not being given to plagiarism, refrained from administering a like rebuke to his annoyer. In giving his impressions of Paris in his *Epistle to the Right Hon. William Pulteney*, written in 1717, the genial satirist wrote:

> But hark! the full orchestra strikes the strings,
> The hero struts, and the whole audience sings;
> My jarring ear harsh grating murmurs wound,
> Hoarse and confused like Babel's mingled sound.
> Hard chance had placed one near a noisy throat,
> That in rough quavers bellowed every note.
>
> " Pray, sir," said I, " suspend awhile your song
> The opera's drowned, your lungs are wondrous strong;
> I wish to hear your Roland's ranting strain,
> When he with rooted forests strews the plain."
> " *Monsieur assurément n'aime pas la musique.*"
> Then turning round, he joined the ungrateful noise,
> And the loud chorus thundered with his voice.

The reference here is to a revival of Lully's *Roland*, which dates from 1685. It is noteworthy that already, some few years before Gay's poem was written, the Franco-Italian comedians had found it necessary, through sheer force of circumstance, to take neat advantage of the native predilection for chorusing. With the view of suppressing their performances at the great annual fairs of

AQUATIC THEATRE, SADLERS WELLS,

BOX 4s.

Nº. 54.

Mª. C. DIBDIN'S NIGHT.

Monday, September 22ᵈ 1817.

DIBDIN'S BENEFIT TICKET, SEPTEMBER 1817

Showing a view of Sadler's Wells.

196

Saint-Germain and Saint-Laurent the Royal Academy of Music, otherwise the monopolists of the *opéra*, made undue exercise of its prerogative and forbade these players from indulging their public with song. Highly ingenious were the methods whereby the persecuted ones evaded this grave prohibition. The comedian who, in the ordinary course, should have sung brought with him, on coming on, a scroll on which was indited in bold letters the words of his song, and which he at once unrolled and displayed to the audience. The song was set to a popular tune, and, the musicians having played it over, a few hired men scattered among the spectators started singing it, and induced the rest of the audience to join in. Afterwards this simple device was somewhat improved upon. Two little Cupids came down from above, supporting an inscribed canvas which unrolled as they descended. The result was that, so far from injuring the players, the Royal Academy of Music had done them a service, for all the world and his wife trooped to see the novelty.[1] Judging, however, by their silence on the point, French theatrical historians are unaware that the device so successfully exploited was not really new. It had been brought from Italy. Writes Hogarth in the opening chapter of his *Memoirs of the Musical Drama* (1838):

> Towards the end of the seventeenth century a species of entertainment was introduced at Venice which was for a short time in great vogue. It consisted of little dramas, in which the actors appeared on the stage without speaking. Scrolls descended from the roof upon their heads in succession, in which were written, in large letters, verses of songs, the airs of which were played by the orchestra, while the words were sung by the spectators; the performers on the

[1] Maurice Albert, *Les Théâtres de la foire* (1900), Chapter III; N.-M. Bernardin, *La Comédie italienne en France* (1902), Chapter III.

stage, meanwhile, carrying on the action in dumb shew. The spectators found it very amusing to sing in this manner the dialogue of the piece, but soon began, doubtless, to think it somewhat childish, for the scroll-pieces did not long remain in fashion.

But if in Italy the device, after amusing a brief hour, passed and left no trace, its adoption in France proved more vital and, in a sense, epoch-marking. To it was due the genesis of the *opéra comique*.

Much has been written in recent times about collective psychology, the 'law of the crowd.' We know now that the aggregate acumen of any considerable mass of people is much less than the sum-total of the intelligence of its component parts. As A. B. Walkley, the dramatic critic, once put it, "the crowd has the credulity, the absence of judicial faculty, the uncontrolled violence of feeling, of a child." Bacon was groping for this idea when he wrote in *De Augmentis*, " and certainly it is most true, and one of the greatest secrets of nature, that the minds of men are more open to impressions and affections when many are gathered together than when they are alone." But in this matter the national equation counts; and it must be borne in mind that we Britons are among the least demonstrative and most repressive of people. To the natural man no impulse is more difficult to resist than the urge to join in a chorus. People like to get immersed in the rhythm of a titillating ditty, just as they like to fall in step. There has been no period in our history when the natural man was more on the surface than in the Elizabethan period, yet one searches the records of that great epoch in vain for any indication that theatre audiences then showed the slightest disposition to raise their voices in unison with the singer. Whether owing to natural reserve or some idea of scenic propriety, spontaneous outbursts of the sort at the play were remarkably long delayed. The first chorusing on record in an English theatre was not chorusing of that order. Early in the eighteenth century it became usual for the members of the Ancient Order of Free and Accepted Masons in London and Dublin to repair to the theatre in full regalia on St John's Day, the period of their annual festivity. On these occasions Masonic songs were sung between the acts by the players and chorused in pit and boxes by the brethren. Thus, of the visit paid by the Irish Free Masons to the Smock Alley Theatre on June 24, 1725, we read in *The Dublin Weekly Journal* of the time:

> They all went to the Play, with their aprons, etc.; the private Brothers sat in the Pit, but the Grand Master and Grand Warden, in the Government Box; at the conclusion of the play Mr Griffith the player, who is a Brother, sang the Free Mason's Apprentice's song, the Grand Master and the whole brotherhood joining in the chorus.

The Government box, it should be noted, was the box occupied by the Lord-Lieutenant on 'command nights,' or, in his absence from the country, by the Lords Justices.

This curious custom lived for long and travelled far afield. There was a Masonic night at the Queen Street Theatre in Charleston, South Carolina, on May 26, 1737, when there was a full attendance at the play of *The Recruiting Officer*. A contemporary report reveals that between the acts the Apprentices' and Masters' songs were sung on the stage and chorused by the brethren in the pit.[1] It is noteworthy, however, that despite the fact

[1] See the New York *Nation* of September 3, 1914, article on "Charleston Theatres, 1735–66."

that subsequent immigration filled her land with a weird mixture of races America so far preserved her initial British tone as never to take kindly to singing at the play. Even in her Halls of Variety all attempts to popularize community singing have failed. In New York, a quarter of a century ago, Vesta Victoria wheedled the audience into raising their voices with hers in *Waiting at the Church*, and, following the innovation, one or two American singers strove to establish the practice, but the response was never more than lukewarm.

There came a time, however, in England when what Dryden had proposed in jest was proposed by another dramatist in earnest. The moment was apparently opportune, for the plea was made just when the immense vogue of *The Beggar's Opera* had established a liking for light musical plays in which all the songs were set to popular tunes. When Colley Cibber's luckless ballad-opera *Love in a Riddle* was produced at Drury Lane in January 1729, Harper, that jolliest of obese comedians, was provided with a ballad-epilogue of four stanzas in which the urge was made:

> Since songs to plays are nowadays,
> Like to your meals a salad,
> Permit us then, kind gentlemen,
> To try our skill by ballad;
> While you, to grace our native lays,
> As France has done before us,
> Belle, beau and cit from box and pit,
> All join the jolly chorus.

The chorus ran:

> Then freeborn boys, all make a noise,
> As France has done before us;
> With English hearts all bear your parts,
> And join the jolly chorus.

ARLEQUIN

C'est lui (puisques ses malheurs)
C'est lui qui le sort baloto .
Reconnoissez-le à ses pleurs,
Caur plus à sa culote .

MEZZETIN . ARLEQUIN . PIERROT .

SCENE FROM LESAGE'S "ARLEQUIN, ROI DE
SERENDIB," AT THE FOIRE DE SAINT-GERMAIN, 1713

Agreeable to command, the freeborn boys in the pit made the devil of a noise, but it was not of the nature suggested. For some obscure reason a cabal had been organized against the little piece, which was mortally wounded on its first night, and expired on its second. With it passed away all possibility of the adoption of the French custom in the English theatre. Masonic chorusing apart, for a full century and more playhouse melody was not to be of the audience's making. Not but that an occasional still small voice was to be heard by quick ears piping up in the house. When Gay's long-prohibited ballad-opera *Polly* was first produced at the Haymarket (in somewhat altered form) in 1777, the author's old patron the venerable Duchess of Queensberry was present. Relative to her visit Mrs John Larpent wrote in her *Diary*:

> *June 25th*. At the play *Polly*, or the second part of *The Beggar's Opera*. I was extremely pleased to go with the Duchess and see the opera, which, from the protection she gave its author Gay and from the spirit of the time, occasioned her dismission from Court. She heard it with delight. She sang all the airs after ye actors.

It was not until the rise of the music-halls in the sixties that John Bull conquered his diffidence and sang up with gusto. One need not express any surprise at the outburst of chorusing that took place there, for the early music-hall was merely a scientific development of the old Free and Easy, where, as its denomination betokens, people unbent and even the staidest were apt on the impulse of the moment to sing with full throats. Such was the prevalence of the custom in the Halls of Variety that it came in time to invade the theatre. Half a century ago it was usual to set all the songs in Christmas pantomime to popular music-hall tunes of the hour, and sheer association of ideas, combined with the Puckish impulsiveness of the holiday spirit, led to occasional chorusing during the performance. That tendency was accentuated later on, when, instead of the customary parodies of music-hall ditties, the ditties themselves were inappropriately introduced. Pantomime performers came in time deliberately to encourage chorusing, and made direct appeals to the audience to induce them to sing. Rarely, however, save at holiday time, did the playgoing public indulge in this practice. As an exceptional instance one recalls that when Walter Howard's romantic play *The Story of the Rosary* was taken round the provinces in 1915 an act-drop was regularly let down during one of the intervals in the performance, having inscribed upon it the words of the song of *The Rosary* on which the play was based, and, with the playing of the haunting melody by the orchestra, the audience was readily induced to sing the song. Such was the genesis of a custom afterwards followed to some extent in the cinemas, where, however, community singing has never enjoyed any particular vogue. It is not to be expected that in a place of darkness, where the performers are shadows, the festive music-hall spirit can obtain.

CHAPTER XXII

THE NUMBERER

EARLY in Restoration times two foolish privileges were unguardedly granted to a certain class of playgoer—possibly under pressure of precedent—which soon gave rise to abuses inimical to the financial well-being of the theatre, and which became so deeply embedded that they resisted eradication for fully three-quarters of a century. It was impolitic enough that frequenters of the boxes should have been allowed to walk into the house unchallenged on the understanding that they were ultimately to pay their money to a collector, but matters became complicated by the establishment of the further privilege that, on the principle of 'taste and try before you buy,' the town gallant was allowed to see one act of the play for nothing. In the beginning it was probably the first act only that he was thus intended to see, but in his high-handed way he insisted on applying the concession to any act, and came in time to extend it to a couple of acts. This led to evasion of payment. Not in all cases when the boxkeeper, as collector, went his rounds could he peremptorily demand payment. He could not always be certain how long the spectator had been in the house, and the usual method of the trickster was to say that he did not purpose remaining, and there and then remove himself to another part of the boxes or another part of the house. The Dublin manager of the period paid his London compeers the sincerest form of flattery, and an abuse that was rife in the Dublin theatre in the first half of the eighteenth century merely echoed what had long been practised in the London theatres. In 1740 one finds Lewis Duval, the controller of old Smock Alley, advertising:

> Whereas complaints have been made that numbers of persons nightly shift from box to box and into the pit, so to the stage, which appears on enquiry that it is to avoid payment, for the future prevention thereof an office is kept for the boxes where all gentlemen are requested to take tickets before they go in.

There is ample evidence that similar tricks had long been practised in the London theatres, but it was not until 1745 that Garrick checked them by emulating Duval's example at Drury Lane. In vain had the satirist striven to quell the prevailing dishonesty. Here, much as I abhor repetition, necessity compels me to cite again some lines from the prologue to Tom D'Urfey's comedy of *The Bath, or The Western Lass*, written in 1701, already given in a former chapter:

> I'm told that Beaux with Perukes cover'd o'er,
> Make such strange shifts to save poor shillings four;
> They'll in Side-Box three Acts for nothing sit,
> At last sneak down for Six-pence to the Pit.

Six years later Archer, in *The Beaux' Stratagem*, while discussing with his friend Aimwell the painful alternative to their rural situation, spoke with disgust of the compulsions of an empty purse, and, among other things, of their being obliged when in town "to sneak into the side-box, and between both houses steal two acts of a play, and because we ha'n't money to see the other three, we come away discontented and damn the whole five." Here the meaning is a trifle obscure. What Archer wished to convey was that when he and his friend were constrained to leave the one house after having seen the first two acts gratis they sallied forth to the other house and stole another two.

A quarter of a century elapses, and still the old practice is going on. Excoriated as they had been for long by prologue-writers, the box-loungers were never quite so witheringly handled as they came to be by Fielding in his *History of the Life of the Late Mr Jonathan Wild the Great* in 1743. Despised by a master-thief for petty thievery, they had surely reached the last stage of degradation:

> A long intimacy and friendship subsisted between the Count and Mr Wild, who, being by the advice of the Count dressed in good clothes, was by him introduced into the best company. They constantly frequented the assemblies, auctions, gaming-tables and playhouses; at which they saw two acts every night, and then retired without paying—this being, it seems, an immemorial privilege which the beaux of the town prescribe for themselves. This, however, did not suit Wild's temper, who called it a cheat, and objected against it as requiring no dexterity, but what every blockhead might put into execution. He said it was a custom very much savouring of the sneaking budge (shop-lifting), but neither so honourable nor so ingenious.

Since nothing short of a severing of the Gordian knot could have prevented the boxkeeper from being cheated, the best that managers could do in the circumstances was to see that they, in their turn, were not cheated by the boxkeeper. To put a check upon him and keep him alert to his duties the office of the numberer was instituted. Exactly at what period this took place cannot now be determined. It was certainly not later than the beginning of the eighteenth century, and may have been considerably earlier. The first numberer on record was one

Knapton, a relative of Wilks, the famous comedian, and we find him in occupation of the post at Drury Lane in 1713, when his salary was 18s. per week. This sounds a meagre stipend, but most of the known numberers pursued some trade, added to which it became usual to give those holding the office an annual benefit, although what they did for the public at large warranting them to appeal to their bounty is difficult to see. In a contemporary report of a theatrical lawsuit in 1713 Knapton is described as " a very useful and necessary person in taking the number of the auditory every night to prevent fraud by the doorkeepers." This is by no means scientifically accurate. No numberer was ever expected to count the whole of the audience. At this particular period, and for some time after, it was the business of the numberer to make a return of the numbers in the front and side boxes only. Where he sat in Knapton's time in order to fulfil his task is an interesting speculation. Benjamin Victor, afterwards to be identified as the first Irish Poet Laureate, tells us that at the first performance at Drury Lane on November 7, 1722, of Steele's *The Conscious Lovers* he sat with the author in " Burton's box," and that the said box was in the centre of the middle gallery. Also that the price of admission to it was the same as to the pit—to wit, half a crown (though seats in the middle gallery cost only eighteenpence).[1] That curious isolated box was for long a feature of the house. In the forty-third number of *The Guardian*, issued on April 20, 1713, " Mary Lizard " is to be found writing: " My brother Tom waited upon us all last night at *Cato*; we sat in the first seats, in the Box of the Eighteen Penny Gallery." Twenty years later a

[1] Benjamin Victor, *Original Letters*, i, 237.

reference occurs to Burton's box in Fielding's *The Miser*. Says Lappet in the opening scene, " About a month ago, my young lady goes to a play in an undress, and takes me with her. We sat in Burton's box," etc. Situated immediately above the front boxes, the middle gallery was one of the cheapest and most unfashionable parts of the house. It was an open amphitheatre, and the popular rendezvous of petty tradesmen and their wives. One cannot believe that a box was erected in its midst primarily for the convenience of the public. We have furthermore to ask ourselves why the box should have been given the name of an individual, and been so long known as Burton's. No other box except the King's box was so identified in the Restoration or post-Restoration theatre. Might it not have been that the box was originally constructed for the numberer, and that, in Drury Lane, Burton was the first man to occupy the post? We shall see later that members of the public were allowed to sit with the numberer in his box.

The curious thing is that traces of a box in the middle gallery can be found at a very early period in the history of the Restoration theatre. Whether or not this points to an early institution of the numberer's office cannot now be determined. When London had but two theatres, the Theatre Royal and the Duke's, both had a middle-gallery box. On February 6, 1668, Pepys repaired to the Duke's as early as two o'clock to see the first performance of *She would if she could*, but found the pit already crowded, " and I at last, because my wife was there, made shift to get into the 18*d*. box, and there saw. . . . The King was there; but I sat mightily behind, and could see but little and hear not at all." On April 15 following we find him going to the Theatre Royal, and "into a corner of the 18*d*. box." So, too, on the succeeding 8th of December he made his way to the Duke's, "where, with much ado, at half-past one, we got into a blind hole in the 18*d*. place, above stairs, where we could not hear well, but the house infinite full."

After Knapton the first numberer to loom into sight was Thomas Arne, a man who now would be utterly forgotten were it not for the fact that he lives in the reflected light of his children's genius. He was the sire of the celebrated Mrs Cibber and the hardly less celebrated composer of *Rule, Britannia!* Arne occupied the post at Old Drury in the Fleetwood *régime*. He was then carrying on a furnishing and undertaking business at the sign of the Two Crowns and Cushions in King Street, Covent Garden, only a stone's-throw from the theatre, and must have found his secondary occupation a pleasant relief from the handling of coffins. By a lucky chance we get an interesting glimpse of him at the trial of Charles Macklin at the Old Bailey in 1735 for the manslaughter of Thomas Hallam, his fellow-actor. I have already spoken of Arne's appearance at that trial as a witness, but I purposely refrained then from speaking of his evidence until I could deal with it here. It throws some light on the system he pursued. After explaining that he was "the numberer of the boxes" at Drury Lane, Arne proceeded to say that on the fateful night in question he delivered his accounts at 8 o'clock in at the property office, and then betook himself to "the scene room, where the players warm themselves, and sat in a chair at the side of the fire." In those days the curtain rose at six o'clock, and by the time Arne's duties had ended the performance was three-quarters over.

At Drury Lane on May 23, 1743, a joint benefit was given to the stage doorkeeper, the numberer, and other officials, with Peg Woffington in the bill as Rosalind. Apparently up to this period there was only one numberer, but a score of years later we learn of two—one for the boxes and one for the pit. Covent Garden had two in 1767, Stables and Forrest, and it is curious to note the difference in their pay. Whereas Stables received 5s. per night, Forrest had to remain content with half a crown. In 1779 Alexander Rice, one of the numberers at this house, also held the post of box bookkeeper at the Haymarket, a dual occupation which afforded no difficulties, since Covent Garden was a winter theatre and the Haymarket a summer one.

After Thomas Arne the only numberer of any note was kindly old John Hardham, who was Garrick's under-treasurer at Drury Lane in 1765, and probably combined the two posts about that period. Since he was a well-to-do man his connexion with the theatre was evidently more of a hobby than a necessity. As a dealer in snuff, noted far and wide for his famous '37' brand, he did a roaring trade at the sign of the Red Lion in Fleet Street, and made a fortune there. On his death in 1772 he left the interest of £22,000 in the 3 per cents. to a woman friend, with reversion to the poor of Chichester, his native city. He was intimate with Collins the poet, and was instrumental in persuading him to ignore the wishes of his father, who was desirous for him to take holy orders. A sympathetic portrait of the old man has been drawn by Isaac Reed in the intermediate issue of the *Biographia Dramatica*:

Mr Hardham was at once a patron and preceptor to many of our candidates for histrionic laurels. He was therefore seldom without embryo Richards and Hotspurs strutting and bellowing in his dining-room, or the parlour behind his shop. The latter of these apartments was adorned with heads of most of the persons celebrated for dramatic excellence, and to these he frequently referred in the course of his instructions.

There is one circumstance, however, in his private character, which deserves a more honourable rescue from oblivion. His charity was extensive in an uncommon degree, and was conveyed to many of its objects in the most delicate manner. On account of his known integrity (for he once failed in business more creditably than he could have made a fortune by it) he was often intrusted with the care of paying little annual stipends to unfortunate women, and others who were equally in want of relief; and he has been known, with a generosity almost unexampled, to continue their annuities long after the sources of them had been stopped by the deaths or caprices of the persons who at first supplied them. At the same time he persuaded the receivers that their money was remitted to him as usual through its former channel.

Henry Angelo, in his *Reminiscences*, tells us that the numberer's box at Old Drury in Hardham's time was "the last box next to the stage, of the very upper boxes, on the prompter's side," and that it projected out from the others like a tub. Having the old man's friendship as a boy, he was always welcomed there, and remembered how Mrs Barry, Mrs Abington, and Miss Young on their off-nights used to sit with Hardham, discreetly shrouded in long black veils. He tells us also that it was customary then to count the house twice, once before the taking of half-price and once after.

CHAPTER XXIII

'ENCORE! ENCORE!'

PLAIN truths are sometimes startling. Encoring is now with us so far a second nature that it comes with a shock of surprise to learn that there was a period of a hundred and thirty years in the history of the English theatre during which no audience ever asked for the repetition of anything. It was not until the dawn of the eighteenth century that the principle of the encore was established in our midst. One can almost fix the date. This curious belatedness was due to the fact that initially encoring was an offshoot of opera, but sprouted only when opera came out into the open. It was the popularization of the new Italian music-drama and its gradual diffusion that sowed the seeds of the custom all over the civilized world. No practice of the sort existed anywhere until the first public opera-houses were established in Venice in the third decade of the seventeenth century.[1] Italy had a monopoly of the principle for long. It cannot well have been established in France until after the opening of the first French opera-house in the rue des Fossés-de-Nesle in Paris in 1671, nor in England until Vanbrugh, in 1705, built a home for Italian opera in the Haymarket. As a matter of fact, so far as our own country is concerned, there is evidence to show that in 1712 it was looked upon

---

[1] See Henry Thomas Riley, *The Comedies of Plautus* (1852), i, 38, note, for a feeble attempt to maintain that encoring was practised in the ancient Roman theatre. Something more will have to be advanced than the vague allusion here referred to before any entertainment can be given to the hypothesis.

as a new fad, something un-English and restricted in its use, and as such fair game for the satirist. Masquerading as one " Toby Rentfree," Steele has a letter to the editor in the 314th number of *The Spectator* in which he asks him to settle a nice point:

> You are to know that I am naturally Brave, and love Fighting as well as any Man in *England*. This gallant Temper of mine makes me extremely delighted with Battles on the Stage. I give you this Trouble to complain to you, that *Nicolini* refused to gratify me in that Part of the Opera for which I have most taste. I observe its becoming a Custom, that whenever any Gentlemen are particularly pleased with a Song, at their crying out *Encore* or *Altro Volto*, the Performer is so obliging as to sing it over again. I was at the Opera the last time *Hydaspes* was performed. At that part of it where the Heroe engages with the Lion, the graceful Manner with which he puts that terrible Monster to Death gave me so great a Pleasure, and at the same time so just a Sense of that Gentleman's Intrepidity and Conduct that I could not forbear desiring a repetition of it, by crying out *Altro Volto* in a very audible Voice; and my friends flatter me, that I pronounced those Words with a tolerably good Accent, considering that it was but the third Opera I had ever seen in my Life. Yet, notwithstanding all this, there was so little Regard had to me, that the Lion was carried off, and went to Bed, without being killed any more that Night. Now, Sir, pray consider that I did not understand a Word of what Mr *Nicolini* said to this cruel Creature; besides I have no Ear for Musick; so that during the long Dispute between 'em, the whole Entertainment I had was from my Eye; why then have I not as much Right to have a graceful Action repeated as another has a pleasing Sound, since he only hears as I only see, and we neither of us know that there is any reasonable thing a-doing? Pray, Sir, settle the Business of this claim in the Audience, and let us know when we may cry *Altro Volto*, *anglicé*, *again*, *again* for the future.

Writing a century ago in his *Musical Memoirs*, Parke was the first to draw attention to the remarkable circumstance that in demanding the repetition of a song the French and the English had each selected for regular use "a word forming no part of their respective languages—the former making use of the Latin word *bis*, and the latter the French word *encore*." A good deal more requires to be said on this point. It is difficult to know how "*Encore!*" came to be the popular cry in England. It was no following of a French fashion, for France has never used the word in the way we use it. What Toby Rentfree's letter particularly reveals is that seven years after the Italian opera-house in the Haymarket was first opened the principle of the encore was in existence there, but there was not then, as later, a solitary method of setting up the demand. We learn from it that both *encore* and *altro volto* were used indifferently for the purpose, and, as it happens, we learn from another issue of *The Spectator* (No. 323, March 11, 1712) that a third term was also in use. This was *ancora*—in all probability the commonest of all. Note what Clarinda is represented as entering in her diary on a Saturday:

Six a-clock. Went to the Opera. I did not see Mr *Froth* till the beginning of the second act. Mr *Froth* talked to a Gentleman in a black Wig. Bowed to a Lady in the front Box. Mr *Froth* and his Friend clapp'd *Nicolini* in the third Act. Mr Froth cried out *Ancora*. . . .

In the struggle for supremacy *ancora* almost won the day. Uses of the term in the ordinary English theatre at a slightly later period are known of, and one is presently to be cited. It seems to me that *encore*, being a syllable shorter and easier to shout, was substituted for it. For long the two terms were certainly confused. One reads in *The Hibernian Journal*, a Dublin paper, of February 24, 1778, that a certain feature in the new locally produced opera of *The Ruling Passion* had been well received on its first night, " and *anchored* by the audience." [1]

The variety of ways in which encoring was practised at the Queen's Theatre in the Haymarket in early days indicates that there was no adoption of the existing Italian method, and it is much to be doubted if any of the terms used had ever been heard in an Italian theatre. Perhaps all that the cultured patrons of the Queen's then cared about was to make themselves readily understood by the foreign singers who came to that house. The term used originally in Italy was *da capo*, and Germany and Portugal were alone in following suit. France adopted *bis* and Spain *repetición*.

In course of time the increase of encoring at the Italian opera-house in the Haymarket proved a nuisance. In 1715 it was deemed necessary to notify the public that " Whereas by the frequent calling for the songs over again the operas have been too tedious; therefore the singers are forbid to sing any song above once, and it is hoped nobody will call for 'em, or take it ill when not obeyed." But not even Mrs Partington's attempt to stay the oncoming of the billows proved more futile. The encore had not only come to stay, but to widen its activities. Again and again the directors of the opera strove ineffectually to check the practice. When *Artaxerxes* was announced for performance on March 30, 1736, it was notified at the bottom of the bill that " whereas the repetition of songs adds considerably to the length of the

---

[1] *Cf.* the Abbé Prévost's account of the fencing-match in London in 1728 between the redoubtable Figg and an Irish soldier in his *Mémoires d'un homme de qualité*, Book V. When the Irishman gave Figg a slash on the arm Figg at once responded by cutting a slice from his leg. " Tout le monde applaudit à un si beau coup en frappant des mains et en criant *bravo, bravo, ancora, ancora*, qui est façon d'applaudir qu'ils ont prise des Italiens."

opera, and has been complained of, it is hoped no person will take it ill if the singers do not comply with encores for the future." Burney,[1] in commenting on this intimation, suggests that things might be equalized by the eliminating of an uninteresting *aria* by an indifferent singer opposite every encore given. The story, he adds, being carried on by the recitative, alterations of the sort would not signify. This was, indeed, what the medical faculty call 'an heroic remedy.'

Throughout the eighteenth century the opera-going public insisted on having its own way in these matters. In 1771, after a notable two years' service at the King's Theatre, Guadagni, one of the greatest lyric artists of his time, was forced to leave England because of the hostility shown towards him through his tacit refusal to abandon his ideas of scenic propriety either by taking an encore or bowing when he was applauded.[2] A little later they were managing things much better in France. Kotzebue, in discussing the revival of Rousseau's *Le Devin du village* at the Académie de Musique in 1804, tells us that an air was actually encored, although the practice rarely occurred at that house.[3]

When Steele, in his *rôle* of Toby Rentfree, viewed the principle of the encore from a dramatic standpoint, and reduced it to absurdity by insisting that he had as much right to demand the repetition of a stage fight as another man had to demand the repetition of a song, he little

---

[1] *History of Music*, iv, 392.
[2] At Drury Lane in 1735 Poitiers, the dancer, through having refused to repeat a dance and assuming an undeferential attitude towards the audience, was compelled by the sovereign authority of the pit to go down on his knees and apologize to the house before he was allowed to resume his duties (Émile Dacier, *Mademoiselle Sallé*, p. 167).
[3] *Souvenirs de Paris en 1804*, ii, 242.

thought how soon it would be demonstrated that his timely ridicule fell on idle ears. In less than a month encoring was to be heard otherwise than in an opera-house—probably for the first time in its history—and for a purpose otherwise than the repetition of a song. Toby Rentfree's desire was only a trifle more absurd than what then happened. When "Namby-Pamby" Philips's tragedy *The Distrest Mother* was produced at Drury Lane on March 17, 1712, the house was so much taken with Mrs Oldfield's delivery of Addison's epilogue that it insisted upon having it all over again. " The second Night," writes Budgell in the 341st *Spectator*,

> the Noise of Ancora's was as loud as before, and she was again obliged to speak it twice: the third Night it was still called for a second time; and, in short, contrary to all other epilogues, which are dropt after the third Representation of the Play, this has already been repeated nine times.

Since epilogues are distinctly ' beyond the work ' it must at least be conceded that these repetitions, senseless as was the impulse that dictated them, were in nowise made at the expense of any theatrical illusion. Of few encorings can as much be said. The danger of such concessions, however, was that they might readily lead to demands for the repetition of speeches in the play proper —a thing, indeed, which eventually happened. We are told in *The Life of Mr James Quin* that when that superb declaimer succeeded Barton Booth at Drury Lane in 1729 as the exponent of Addison's *Cato* his acting proved so acceptable that " when he repeated the famous soliloquy he was *encored* to that degree, that, though it was sub-mitting to an impropriety, he indulged the audience with its repetition." That particular sort of impropriety never developed into a custom, but it recurred at intervals for a full century. Somehow one's opinion of the ill-taste of the old public becomes mitigated on learning that even such an artistic-minded people as the French erred occasionally in the same way. But further instances of these lapses require to be recorded, if only to show how long the salutary law of the invisible fourth wall had to struggle before gaining any sure foothold.

In Tony Aston the younger's satirical ballad-opera *The Stage Mutineers, or A Playhouse to be Let*, as produced at Covent Garden in October 1733, there was a good deal of trenchant girding at the squabbling of the contemporary player-folk, and among those lampooned the lash fell heaviest on Theophilus Cibber, that unhappy son of a celebrated father. He was felicitously featured as Ancient Pistol. Curious to see himself as others saw him, Theophilus betook himself one evening to the theatre, and, out of sheer bravado, planted himself conspicuously in a side-box. In a sham autobiography of the wight purporting to have come from his own pen the following account is given of what ensued:

> Well, the scene opened, and on Pistol's appearing there was a thundering clap, and all the eyes in the house converted on me every sentence that hit me; the joke was heightened by looking at me, who laughed as much as them. Towards the last scene the author had introduced a sale of theatrical goods, and one of the properties to be disposed of was Apollo's cracked harp and withered crown of bays; upon which a character on the stage replied, "Oh! pray lay that aside for Mr Pistol; he will claim that by hereditary right!" This immediately put the whole house in a roar, and "*Encore! Encore!*" was all the cry. Here the whole pit stood up and looked at me. I joined the laughing encore, and in the repetition of the low witticism clapped heartily.

Players in those days, no matter what their station or sex, had to do as they were bid. The time was not very far ahead when a theatre would be wrecked because actors refused to repeat a speech in a play. This happened in Dublin in 1754, at a time of great political excitement. The game of politics has always been taken seriously in Ireland, but never, perhaps, more seriously than then. Dublin was divided into two hostile camps, the Court party, headed by the Duke of Dorset, then Viceroy and wholly West British in sentiment, and the Country party, whose interests were solely in Ireland. The maltreated island was already groaning under the burden of an iniquitous pension list (on which most of the beneficiaries were outlanders), but, as if this was not *quantum sufficit*, Dorset was scheming to make Ireland's depleted exchequer contribute to the reduction of England's National Debt. This was the summons to arms. The patriots called up all their resources, and when the Money Bill was introduced into the Commons on December 17, 1753, for the purpose it was defeated by five votes. So far from being content to rest on their laurels, the victors were only emboldened by their triumph to pursue their vigilance.

No opportunity was lost to score against their rivals. The misfortune was that the players were drawn unwittingly into the entanglement. After having for some time contemplated the revival of Miller's tragedy of *Mahomet the Impostor*, Thomas Sheridan, the actor-manager of Smock Alley, announced its production for Saturday, February 2, 1754, and immediately the patriots began perusing the play with the view of finding which passages could be vehemently applauded by way of reflection on their opponents. Smock Alley had been experiencing a dull time, but the revival, on its first night, drew a crowded house, with the Irish Irelanders in full muster in the pit. There was a distinguished cast: Sheridan was the Zaphna, Digges the Alcanor, and Peg Woffington the Palmira. In the first act the patriots pounced with avidity on Alcanor's outburst:

> If, ye powers divine!
> Ye mark the movements of this nether world,
> And bring them to account, crush, crush those vipers,
> Who, singled out by the community
> To guard their rights, shall, for a grasp of ore,
> Or paltry office, sell them to the foe.

This evoked from them a burst of applause, followed by imperative cries of "*Encore!*" Unaware that there was any precedent for such a demand (which had certainly never previously been made in Ireland), Digges was puzzled for a moment what to do, but, the cries continuing, he yielded to the apparent wishes of the house and gave the speech again. Thenceforth, although to Sheridan and Peg Woffington fell the finest scenes in the play, he was the bright particular star of the evening, and the only player to gain any applause.

What was Sheridan to do in the conditions? He was well known to be a strong adherent of the Court party, and after having unwittingly given a handle to the enemy, it was not his interest to give further performances of the play. But, being as tactless and as much prone to blundering as his father before him, he did precisely the wrong thing. Because demands were subsequently set up in the house for a repetition of the tragedy he weakly complied, and announced its second performance for the 2nd of March. Nothing if not sententious, on the day previous he assembled all the members of his company in the green room of the theatre and read them a homily on the prime duties of a player.[1] He very properly deprecated the introduction of party feeling into the theatre, and pointed out that it was not the business of people of their profession to give any encouragement to it. Encoring of speeches he deemed (as we have seen, incorrectly) a complete innovation, and one to be sturdily resisted. He spoke of the disadvantages of conceding such liberties, of the disorder which must inevitably ensue, but, strange to say, neither he nor the Press of the hour made any reference to such encoring as a grave scenic impropriety. But as he made no definite ruling and was cautious enough not to take upon himself the onus of responsibility, his assembling of the company was a grave error of judgment, and did more harm than good. He concluded his address by saying:

> "To you, Mr Digges, I must particularly apply, as you were the first tragedian I ever heard of who repeated a speech upon the encore of an audience. I am in hopes it was the suddenness of the thing, and want of time to reflect upon the ill-consequences which might attend it. You have now heard my arguments on that head; if you think they are of weight I suppose you will act accordingly; if not, remember I do not give you any orders upon this occasion: you are left entirely free to act as you please."

Digges, not caring to shoulder any responsibility in the matter, at once arose and asked point-blank what he was to do if the speech was again encored. Sheridan, in reply, shabbily temporized, and told him to act on his own judgment. "Then, sir," said Digges, "if I should

[1] For a copy of the address see Robert Hitchcock, *An Historical View of the Irish Stage*, i, 232–240.

comply with the demand of the audience and repeat the speech, am I to incur your censure?" To which the answer was, "Not at all; I leave you to act in that matter as you think proper."

But when news of the meeting leaked out Sheridan gained nothing by his shilly-shallying. The patriots had made up their minds to encore the speech again, and in the event of non-compliance to hold him responsible. The second night came, and with it another full house. Digges, on the speech being encored, came forward and respectfully addressed the audience. He told them that it had been agreed upon by the company that any repetition of a speech in a play was a prostitution of the stage. He expressed his distress at having to choose between offending a public for which he had the greatest possible respect and acting improperly, but, in the conditions, he was compelled to refuse the request. At once a strident cry was set up for Sheridan, but Sheridan's only response was to lower the curtain and send on the prompter to say that if they were prepared to hear the rest of the play in quiet the performance would go on, or they could have their money back. The prompter duly delivered his message, but nobody heard it in the din. At this juncture Sheridan's courage, like Bob Acres', oozed out of his finger-tips, and, fearing personal assault, he hastily disrobed and, in spite of all remonstrances, left the theatre.

Somebody then appeared before the curtain and volunteered to read Zaphna's part, so that the play might go on, but the audience was in no mood for compromise and hooted him off. Next Peg Woffington sallied forth with the hope of exercising her blandishments, but, in despite of her abounding popularity, she could gain no hearing. As a last resource, Digges, under the persuasion of his fellow-players, reappeared, and, being respectfully received, explained that Sheridan was not directly responsible for his refusal to give the encore, and should not, therefore, incur their displeasure. All to no purpose: the patriots were determined on humiliating Sheridan by way of punishing him for his allegiance to the Court party. They demanded that he be sent for, and said that they would wait an hour for his return. Messengers were sent out in hot haste, and found the much-perturbed manager cooling his heels under his own roof-tree. But he was adamant, and refused to budge a yard. When the hour had expired and still no Sheridan the malcontents went about their business very methodically. First came the stormy petrels, two dignified gentlemen in the pit, who repaired to the boxes and, with the utmost politeness, handed out all the ladies. Then the signal for riot was given in a curious way: a young patriot arose in the middle of the pit and called for three cheers for his Majesty King George. The last huzza had hardly died away before the audience fell to its work of destruction, with such zeal that within a quarter of an hour the whole auditorium was a sorry wreck. What hands failed to do swords accomplished. Benches were torn up and broken, candelabra shattered, and the hangings of the boxes cut to ribbons. Then a rush was made for the stage by the sword-flourishing rioters, who rent the expensive curtain in twain and partially set it on fire. But for the fact that the stage carpenters had taken time by the forelock and barricaded the way to the wardrobe many rich dresses would also have been destroyed.

Finding nothing more to vent their fury upon, the patriots then went contentedly home. But this was not the end. When the patriots withdrew the mob broke in and proceeded to steal everything they could lay their hands upon. Excellent firewood was to be had free, gratis, and for nothing. Some of the rabble, on mischief bent, repaired to the box-room and drew the large grate out into the middle of the floor, and tried to set fire to the theatre by heaping benches and fragments of wainscot on to the flames. But for the courage of half a dozen stage-hands in attacking the mob and driving them out of the house, not only old Smock Alley, but several houses adjoining, most assuredly would have been burned down. Once having got rag, tag, and bobtail outside and barricaded the doors, the dauntless sextet scattered them like chaff by firing upon them from the windows. For six mortal hours the rioting had lasted, and in all that time, anxiously as they were sought for about town, not a single peace officer could be found.

That maleficent encore deflected the whole course of Irish theatrical history. Sheridan at once publicly relinquished his control of Smock Alley and went into exile. He let the theatre for a couple of years to Benjamin Victor, his treasurer, and Sowdon, a well-to-do actor and money-lender. They inherited the dregs of his misfortunes, but by dint of giving the patriots rope enough they hung themselves. After their first season had proceeded for a month or two quietly on its way they were alarmed one night by a demand from the pit for the revival of *Mahomet*, and, finding that there were no dissentients, promised that after the lapse of a fortnight for preparation the play would be given. Accordingly, on March 4, 1755, Miller's tragedy was put up, with Gwinnap in Digges' old part of Alcanor. All passed off well. A half-filled house encored the trouble-giving speech, and the encore was responded to. Subsequently another performance of the play was requested and acceded to, but on the night fixed upon there was so miserable an attendance at seven o'clock (little more than £5 having been taken) that the house was dismissed. It was a question of a plague o' both your parties, for the ladies, fearing riot and disorder, had on both nights avoided the theatre.

So far as Ireland was concerned, an ugly precedent had been set up, but happily, political crises being few and far between, it was rarely taken advantage of. But there were two belated recurrences, unattended, however, by any unpleasantness—the first at the Theatre Royal, Crow Street, on February 24, 1778, when Leonard MacNally's comic opera *The Ruling Passion* was produced there for the first time on any stage. A paragraph in *The Hibernian Journal* of March 2 draws attention to the fact that:

> The satirical strokes against the Local Tax in the new comic opera of *The Ruling Passion* had a most happy effect on the first night of the representation, several gentlemen being then in the boxes who were just come from throwing out the Bill in the House of Commons. The speech was extremely well spoken by Mr Dubellamy, and anchored by the audience.

The second recurrence took place in the same theatre on June 21, 1793, when Pope the tragedian and his wife began a starring engagement there in *Jane Shore*. In the course of a letter written to her London friend Mrs Mathew on July 6 we find Mrs Pope saying:

> We have acted six nights, *Jane Shore* first, a *very great* house, *well received*, and Pope's speech to *Gloster* twice repeated,

which I think proves in a great degree the loyalty of the people.

Gloster's speech, thus :

> What if some patriot, for the public good
> Should vary from your scheme—new mould the State?

> HASTINGS. Curse on the innovating hand that
>   'tempts it !
> Remember him, the villain, righteous Heaven,
> In thy great day of vengeance: blast the traitor
> And his pernicious counsels; who for wealth,
> For power, the pride of greatness, or revenge,
> Would plunge his native land in civil wars.

It is impossible to describe the effect this speech had on the audience. I think you would have been gratified to have heard it; it is the first time a speech in a tragedy was ever repeated. Perhaps it proves the loyalty of this city.[1]

It is curious that within forty years memories of *Mahomet* should have been so far forgotten that Mrs Pope could speak of this occurrence as unprecedented. Half a century later demands from a Dublin audience for the repetition of a passage appear to have been set up only as a stern rebuke to the speaker. Dealing with her visit to Ireland in 1851 in her memoirs, Anna Cora Mowatt, the American actress, dwells upon the delightful responsiveness of the Dublin audience, but adds :

> In spite of their readiness to be pleased, they are also alarmingly despotic, and their chiding is often merciless. With some of Shakespeare's plays they are so conversant that, if an actor makes a mistake in the text, they will correct him with a rebuke, and force him to repeat the passage.

Times have indeed changed. It is long since the Dublin, or any other, audience had the capability to indulge in any such chiding.

[1] For the whole letter see J. T. Smith, *A Book for a Rainy Day* (1905), p. 164.

In other countries as well as Ireland there have been occasions when the sudden upwelling of patriotic sentiment has brought about a sad rupture of scenic illusion. When so taken even French audiences have made no bones about encoring a speech. In his *An Actor's Note-book* Frank Archer relates an experience of his while present at the Théâtre-Français on July 18, 1870, just as war had been declared with Prussia. The play was the *Lion amoureux* of Ponsard, and at the close of one of Bressant's great speeches as Humbert there was a tumult of applause, followed by cries for a repetition. Although evidently much surprised at the demand, Bressant came forward and gave a second delivery of the long speech.

In what particular ways the French were given to the employment of the encore a few years later is revealed in the elucidation of the word *bis* in Bouchard's *La Langue théâtrale* :

> **Bis.** Cri, synonyme de ' répétez,' poussé par le public à la suite d'un morceau de chant ou d'un couplet. Ce cri varie beaucoup, suivant le lieu et l'époque. Tout ce qui attaque les classes supérieures est *bissé* dans les théâtres populaires ; ce qui attaque le pouvoir est *bissé* partout. Jadis tout couplet farci de chauvinisme était *bissé* avec frénésie : c'était le bon temps des colonels du *Gymnase* et celui du grand succès de la *Cocarde tricolore* ; la fibre patriotique était encore tendue. Aujourd'hui on demande *bis* pour *Le Pied qui r'mue*, ou *A Chaillot*. C'est un signe des temps.

Although there was a time when our public was much given to the calling for topical addresses—as in 1755, when we were at war with France and Garrick had frequently to comply with demands for the delivery of his prologue to Mallet's masque of *Britannia*—English audiences have never been prone either in periods of political excitement or patriotic fervour to yield to the impulse of the moment and clamour for the repetition of fortuitously allusive speeches in plays. Yet with much less excuse encores of the sort have been given. When Charles Mathews played Mawworm in *The Hypocrite* at the Lyceum in 1809 he interpolated into the part a mock sermon which has been described as the most successful effort of 'gag' ever known. Two years later, on July 1, 1811, when the great mimic played the part in Liverpool, he was astonished by the effect made by the sermon. " I was quite unprepared," he writes,

> for such uproarious demonstrations of delight, and at a loss to account for their expression—roars of laughter, cries of bravo, and at length *encore*. This was the first time the speech had been so honoured (though the precedent was followed in London on my return).[1]

The explanation was that a highly popular dissenting preacher named Spencer was drawing crowds in Liverpool at the time, and Mathews, in caricaturing the type, had all unknowingly given a close imitation of the individual. Mathews afterwards furnished Liston with a copy of the sermon, and Liston, when he delivered it as Mawworm, was always encored. Such, indeed, was Liston's vogue in the character that it caused Mathews to reflect grimly on the ephemerality of an actor's fame. He had been repeatedly amused by questions on the subject, such as, " Did you ever see Liston as Mawworm? " and " Of course you have heard him preach his sermon? I'm told there never was anything but a song encored before that speech. Is it true that he was the first that ever thought of it, and that it is not in the play? "

Behind the scenes there has never been a complete

---

[1] *Life and Correspondence of Charles Mathews* (ed. Yates, 1860), p. 150.

unanimity of opinion as to the advisability of accepting encores. Most theatrical artists take a request for a repetition of a song as a compliment, but some comply grudgingly, looking upon the thing simply as extra labour and a few fail to respond. Managers and singers are not always in agreement upon the point. When the long-popular comic opera of *Dorothy* was transferred to the Prince of Wales's Theatre early in 1887 in the midst of its long run Mr Ben Davies took up the part of Geoffrey Wilder, and one night so highly offended his manager H. J. Leslie, by refusing to accept an encore that he fined him for what he considered a dereliction of duty. Elsewhere, it may be noted, there have been houses of song in which encores were forbidden. For long this rule strictly applied in the Colon Grand Opera House, Buenos Aires, first opened in 1908. But on July 31, 1915, Titla Ruffo, a favourite baritone, made such a sensation by his rendering of the Drinking Song in *Hamlet* that he turned to the stage box in which the President of the Republic sat and looked beseechingly for permission to repeat the song. Much to the delight of the audience a nod gave consent.

CHAPTER XXIV

STAGE SENTINELS

GREED, like vaulting ambition, is apt to overreach itself. It is pitiful to find that under its recurrent urgings our early players were foolish enough to commit the one ugly blunder twice, and, after having unwittingly made a rod for their own backs, and being compelled by royal mandate to repair their fault, had gained so little wisdom by sad experience that they could relapse into their old folly, and by so doing put a break on dramatic progress for fully half a century. The custom of allowing the self-exploiting gallants of Elizabethan times to infest the stage not only, in Marston's phrase, "wronged the general eye very much," but proved obstructive to the traffic of the scene. It is custom, however, rather than conscience, that makes cowards of us all, and no one had the hardihood to attempt the belling of the cat until the second Stuart near the close of his reign took the matter in hand and issued an order forbidding the presence of spectators on the stage.

When the new type of theatre came in with the Restoration attempts were made to renew the bad old practice, and that in despite of the fact that there was now a definite pictorial background to injure; but Old Rowley, having so far innovated as to constitute himself the first English monarch to go publicly to the play, saw to it that there was no backsliding. Again and again he took occasion to reissue his father's mandate. But, alas, in the last decade of the century, when the morose, unsociable, and anæmic Dutchman in occupation of the throne was wholly apathetic in his attitude towards the theatre, and within it a spirit of rank commercialism sprang up, overriding all other considerations, the players, who still participated in the profits, returned dog-wise to their vomit. With the bloods of the town haunting the wings, disorder ensued and the provision of a military guard became essential. Much to the outraging of scenic illusion, an armed grenadier was stationed on either side of the proscenium throughout the performance. Since he was doing sentry go he was in nowise expected to concern himself with the action on the stage, but as acting in those days was kept for the most part well to the front he was apt on occasion to get absorbed in the play, and by his naïve manifestation of emotion to afford supplementary amusement to the audience. A story of Drury Lane told by Steele in the nineteenth issue of *The Guardian* is not only illustrative of this, but, seeing that it was published early in 1713, enables us to make close approximation to the period when the stage sentinels first went on duty. It runs as follows :

It was a cause of great sorrow and melancholy to me some nights ago at a play to see a crowd in the habits of the gentry of England stupid to the noblest sentiment we have. The circumstance happened in the scene of distress betwixt Piercy and Anna Bullen in Banks' popular tragedy of *Virtue Betrayed*. One of the sentinels who stood on the stage, to prevent the disorders which the most unmanly race of young men that ever was seen in any age frequently raise in public assemblies, upon Piercy's beseeching to be heard, burst into tears, upon which the greater part of the audience fell into a loud and ignorant laughter, which others, who were touched with the liberal compassion in the poor fellow, could

THACKERAY'S IMAGINARY SKETCH OF THE VISIT OF QUEEN VICTORIA AND THE
PRINCE CONSORT TO COVENT GARDEN ON THEIR MARRIAGE IN 1840

Below is a beefeater's head.

hardly suppress by their clapping. But the man, without the least confusion of shame in his countenance for what had happened, wiped away the tears, and was still intent upon the play. The distress still rising, the soldier was so much moved that he was obliged to turn his face from the audience, to their no small merriment. Piercy had the gallantry to take no notice of his honest heart, and, as I am told, gave him a crown to help him in his affliction. It is certain this poor fellow, in his humble condition, had such a lively compassion as a soul unwedded to the world; were it otherwise, gay lights and dresses, with appearance of people of fashion and wealth, to which his fortune could not be familiar, would have taken up all his attention and admiration.

Theatrical anecdote, more than any other kind, has seductive adaptiveness—the main reason why it is so rarely credible—and it proves both amusing and instructive to trace the variants of Steele's sentimental theme. A writer in *The Universal Spectator* in 1742 unblushingly retells the story as a personal experience of a few years back, while witnessing the tragedy of *Venice Preserved* at Old Drury, and dwells on the agonizing emotion experienced by the unsophisticated grenadier. Evidently, however, by his time the price of real tears had gone up, for he ends by saying:

> The spectators were so much affected with the fellow's simple, honest heart, that they applauded him with a loud clap. But when a noble duke (then the head of the army) who was behind the scenes, heard of it, he then sent for him and gave him a guinea, telling the gentlemen around him he was sure he was an honest and brave fellow.

So bounteous a reward was enough to raise a regiment of lachrymose grenadiers, and may have tended somewhat towards that end, but if that were the case over-supply brought about a sad depreciation of the return. Note

how John Thomas Smith tells the story in his engrossing
Book for a Rainy Day:

> On a night when Mr Garrick was acting the part of Lear
> one of the soldiers who stood on the stage blubbered like a
> child. Mr Garrick, who was as fond of a compliment as
> most men, when the play was over, sent for the man and
> gave him half a crown.

Not all the stories told, however, about the old stage
grenadiers harp solely on the one string. There is one
noteworthy exception.[1] In a letter written to a friend
in 1740, after he had paid a visit to Covent Garden to
see Rich's pantomime of *Orpheus and Eurydice*, César de
Saussure gives a glowing account of the thrills of the
evening, not the least of which was created by a wonderful mechanical serpent:

> The serpent that killed Eurydice is of enormous size; and
> is covered all over with gold and green scales and with red
> spots; his eyes shine like fire, and he wriggles about the
> stage with head upraised, making an awful but very natural
> hissing noise. The first night this pantomime was given the
> King was here, and I had the good fortune to be present.
> One of the two grenadiers of the guard, who are posted at
> either side of the stage with their backs turned to the players,
> noticed the serpent only when he was at his foot, and the
> reptile was so natural that the man dropped his musket, and,
> drawing his sword, made as though he would cut the
> monster in two. I do not know whether the soldier was
> really alarmed, or whether he was acting, but if so, it was
> admirably done, and the spectators laughed again and again.

Can it have been that the thing was prearranged, a
device of the astute Mr Rich to accentuate the illusion
by pressing the normally stolid grenadier into the service

---

[1] Perhaps one should say two. According to Malcolm's *Manners and Customs*
a sentinel on guard in a London theatre in October 1763, while *Twelfth Night*
was being played, laughed so heartily over the acting of Sir Andrew Aguecheek
that he fell in convulsions on the boards.

of the stage? Hardly so, and yet, somewhere about the same period, say, a lustrum later, that enterprising dramatist Aaron Hill conceived a somewhat similar idea, though the project does not seem to have been put into execution. He wrote a prologue for delivery by Peg Woffington, intended " to be spoken in the new Blue Uniform," in the course of which she was to stride over to one of the red-coated stage guards and shake him warmly by the hand. For some reason that handclasp was never given, but when Hill's collected works came to be published in 1758 the aborted prologue found its way into print.

Since the old Dublin theatre for long took its cue from the sister capital, and the same necessity existing, there is good reason to believe that the principle of the stage sentinel was adopted at Smock Alley not many moons after it had been instituted. It is not, however, until 1729 that we get any proof of its existence there. One evening in the November of that year, when Dublin's sole theatre was occupied by a fashionable audience, including Lady Carteret, the Viceroy's wife, a drunken roysterer came on to the stage shortly after the rising of the curtain, and sat down without taking the trouble to remove his hat. The house resented this act of impoliteness, and expressed its disapprobation accordingly, but the offender's only response was to gaze around defiantly and indulge in a vulgar gesture of contempt. In this he went a trifle too far: he was at once arrested by one of the sentries and hustled unceremoniously into the street.

In the *Apology* for her life (somewhat needed) George Anne Bellamy relates an incident of a much graver order which happened in the same theatre in 1746, shortly after Tom Sheridan, its manager, had given strict orders that no one unconnected with the house was to be allowed behind the scenes. One night, after a severe illness, she had repaired to Smock Alley to see the play, and, as luck would have it, had a very painful experience:

> It happened one night, just as I was so far recovered as to venture to the house, but not to perform, that an officer, who had more wine in his head than humanity in his heart, insisted on passing the sentry placed at the stage door.[1] The poor fellow, persisting in his refusal of admittance, the officer drew his sword and stabbed him in the thigh with such violence that the weapon broke and left a piece in the most dangerous part. Hearing a riot on the stage, I ran from the box in which I sat, and flew in my fright to the nearest sentinel for protection. This happening to be the man who had been wounded, I found myself in a moment encompassed by numbers, and I was obliged to be a witness to the broken steel being taken out.

Though with Sheridan's unwavering determination not to allow outsiders any further admission behind the scenes there was much less necessity for the presence of the stage sentinels, yet it was deemed advisable that they should still remain. Riots in the theatre were not uncommon, and there was always a risk in time of riot of the young bucks and bloods of the town climbing up on to the stage and wantonly destroying the scenery. It had been done.

Once, and once only, in the Irish capital officers condescended to figure on the stage as guards. When the boys of Sam Whyte's famous grammar school gave a performance of Addison's *Cato* at the Crow Street Theatre on January 2, 1772, on behalf of the debtors confined in the several marshalseas, Captain French and Captain Tisdall—

---

[1] By which she means, not the exterior entrance, as the term now applies, but one of the proscenium doors. The context fully substantiates this reading.

the former of whom was himself an excellent amateur actor and a notable Scrub in *The Beaux' Stratagem*—signalized the occasion by doing sentry-go at the stage doors. So far as Ireland was concerned, this was one of the expiring flickers of the old custom, for not long afterwards the stage sentinels disappeared. As they were blots upon the picture it is curious that some one who was apparently a constant playgoer should have wanted them restored. In November 1776 a correspondent of *The Freeman's Journal* ventured to jog the memory of Tom Ryder, that versatile genius who was then conducting Smock Alley, in the following way:

> The Theatre Spy begs leave to remind the manager of the Theatre Royal of his intention to station guards upon the stage. However ludicrous the appearance of these unanimated statues, if this regulation be neglected, Mr Ryder and his company will ever be liable to be annoyed and insulted by the academic spirits and city bloods of this exclusive metropolis.

How the stage guards could have prevented the academic spirits and the young bloods from insulting the players if they remained in their own part of the house said deponent sayeth not. Perhaps it was because his reasoning was not very cogent that his reminder fell on deaf ears. The truth was that the Dublin theatre had once more taken its cue from the sister metropolis. In or about the year of grace 1768 the London players had contrived to get rid of their Old Man of the Sea, and were thankfully able to boast a clear stage and every favour. But oddly enough, though that meant the end of the stage sentinel as a regular institution, it by no means marked the end of the stage guard. There is an interesting sequel to the story. Even as late as the beginning of the nineteenth century a military guard still attended at the King's Theatre in the Haymarket, but it was discreetly placed out of sight, between the wings. There was a reason for this precaution, seeing that there were doors in the pit leading to the stage, and that between the acts subscribers were permitted to hob-nob with the singers and dancers. Writing of a disturbance which took place in this house in 1813, John Ebers says in his *Seven Years of the King's Theatre*:

> Some years previous to my commencement, a considerable disturbance had arisen in the theatre from a part of the company who had been admitted to the stage coming too forward during the representation. The audience before the curtain signified their disapprobation; the effect of which was that the intruders advanced still more; and one or two individuals were so ill-advised as to insult the audience by the most contemptuous gestures. One of the guard, which was then always stationed behind the scenes, struck a bystander with his bayonet. A hurricane immediately ensued; loud cries demanded the expulsion of the offenders; and, the tumult becoming universal, the chairs were flung out of the boxes, chandeliers broken, and property to a great extent destroyed. Complaints were made to the Chamberlain, and his Lordship directed that the stage doors should be closed.

But the visible stage sentinel was hard to kill. Though he disappeared as an institution, after a considerable interval he recurred as an individual. One makes this distinction because his final appearances were made only on red-letter nights. Stage history fails to tell us when it became customary in connexion with royal visits to the theatre to place a guard of honour beneath the royal box. In all probability the practice began immediately after Hadfield's attempted assassination of George III at Drury Lane on May 15, 1800. A striking contemporary engraving of the event shows that no guard was then present.

COMMAND PERFORMANCE OF "LA FIGLIA DEL REGGIMENTO" AT THE ITALIAN
OPERA HOUSE, 1843

236

Curiously enough, the practice had been foreshadowed in the United States of America. When General Washington went to the play in the seventeen-nineties he was ushered to his box over the stage by the manager with all the ceremony usually accorded to crowned heads in England, and a soldier was posted at each proscenium door, and remained on duty throughout the performance.

But it is not until 1825 that we have any definite evidence of the provision of a royal stage guard in the English theatre. When, in that year, Pierce Egan's *The Life of an Actor* fell from the press it was adorned with a composite, semi-allegorical coloured frontispiece, the upper part of which, a vision in the clouds—inscribed " Theatre Royal. The Actor's Climax. Royalty witnessing the Efforts of Genius "—depicts a scene on the stage from *The First Part of Henry IV*, and shows royalty peeping from an upper stage box, and two beefeaters standing on guard immediately below on the verge of the apron. Contrary to the earlier custom, no guard is to be seen on the opposite side of the stage. Such remained the practice on the occasion of royal visits. A view published in *The Illustrated London News* in June 1843, commemorating the recent visit of Queen Victoria and the Prince Consort to the Italian opera-house to see *La Figlia del Reggimento*, bears this out. On another occasion when the Queen honoured the same house with her presence an amusing incident occurred. A diversified programme was provided, and part of it was the farce of *The Spitalfields Weaver*, with Wright, the popular Adelphi comedian, in his favourite *rôle* of Simmons. So far from feeling perturbed by the august presence, Wright was in high fettle, and committed the supreme audacity. When he made his first appearance he looked about perplexedly, puzzled to know where to hang his hat. Then a bright idea struck him. He lumbered over to where the two beefeaters stood beneath the royal box, and quietly placed his beaver on top of one of their halberds. This was funny beyond words, but the point of the story is that neither of the sturdy Yeomen of the Guard moved an eyebrow. What the Queen thought of the liberty taken is not on record, but there was not much opportunity for further pranks of the sort, for after her widowhood she abandoned all public playgoing, and her self-denial on this score wrote *finis* to the long story of the stage sentinel.

CHAPTER XXV

SPECTATORS IN THE ORCHESTRA

IT is a curious fact that there is no part of the theatre from which a sight and hearing of the performance can be obtained but has been frequented at one time or other by members of the audience. We know that in Shakespeare's day the gallants not only incommoded the players by occupying stools on the rush-strewn boards, but were likewise accustomed to sit in elevated boxes at the back of the stage. That, however, is a twice-told tale. Much less knowledge exists, even among theatrical antiquaries, concerning the later custom of allowing spectators to view the performance from the orchestra. It is an interesting speculation how, with us, the practice could have originated. Inspiration may have come from France, where it apparently had its inception, and with far-reaching consequence. At the Théâtre-Français from 1689, as Blondel's ground-plan of the house clearly shows,[1] the stage and the standing *parterre* were separated by an enclosure running from side to side, of which the musicians occupied only a cup-shaped and central partitioned part comprising about a third of the entire space. On the right and left were benches on which certain privileged spectators sat. Originally these seats were monopolized by the Grooms of the Royal Chamber, but some time early in the eighteenth century accommodation was found for them elsewhere, and their old rendezvous became the

[1] See p. 29.

haunt of news-letter writers and dramatists free of the house. As time passed many ordinary members of the public became bitten with a desire to sit in these conspicuous places, and offered money for the privilege. To these importunities the players yielded, permitting seats to be secured there in advance, and taken bodily possession of by servants, with the result that the orchestral benches became so frequented that extra rows had to be added from time to time to cope with the demand. At the Théâtre-Français in 1743 accommodation was afforded in this particular way for close on fifty people.[1] There was gradual encroachment on the standing pit, which was pushed farther and farther back. Hence the origin of the *fauteuils d'orchestre*, or the part of the house in the French theatre corresponding to our present-day stalls.

Though the orchestra well had become permanently established in all the London theatres by the end of the seventeenth century,[2] it had nothing of the nature of the *banc formidable* (to use, for once, the mysterious name by which the extra French benches were known). There was no initial temptation to give accommodation to spectators there, since England had long forestalled France in providing a seated pit. But there was a curious analogy between the position occupied by the French musicians and that occupied by the English, both being centrally situated. Pictorial evidence reveals that the early eighteenth-century English orchestra well was bow-shaped, and occupied only about two-thirds of the width of the

[1] See *The Case of our Present Theatrical Disputes freely stated* (London, 1743), p. 36.
[2] See my illustrated article on "The English Theatre Orchestra: its Rise and Early Characteristics," in *The Musical Quarterly* (New York) for January 1917, iii, 9 ff.

FRONTISPIECE TO PIERCE EGAN'S "THE LIFE OF AN ACTOR"

stage. But, comparatively small as it was, it allowed room for a spectator or two. No doubt the harpsichord at which the leader presided took up a good deal of room, but the musicians were few, not more than six or seven, there being then no brass or drums in the normal theatre orchestra and little, if any, wood-wind.

It cannot now be determined exactly when or how, with us, the custom of allowing others besides the musicians to sit in the orchestra well began, but, seeing that it apparently originated in France, it is curious to note that our first trace of it is associated with the most distinguished Frenchman of his century. When Voltaire visited England for the second time in 1726, to make, as it happened, a lengthened stay, he spent much of his time profitably at the play, and was especially eager to see as much as possible of Shakespeare. Heartily welcomed at Drury Lane as a most desirable guest, he was regularly received at the stage door by Chetwood, the prompter, who provided him with a book of the play and ushered him to his seat in the orchestra. In this way, as well as by concurrent study, he made great advance in his knowledge of English, so much so that within six months he was enabled to correspond in our language with remarkable facility.

It would appear that in those days it was customary for any of the triumvirate of actor-managers then in control of Old Drury who wanted to see a play in which they did not personally figure to repair to 'the musick room,' as the orchestra well was then called. It is on record that on the first night of Mallet's *Eurydice* at Drury Lane (February 22, 1731) Robert Wilks, after delivering the prologue, betook himself thither for the rest of the evening. Writing to Mallet on the day following, Aaron Hill said:

I was truly pleased with Mr Wilks in the prologue, and still more in the musick room, where I observed him aptly and generously touched with a manly and compassionate tenderness; which gave me as strong an esteem for him as ever I drew from the vivacity, the grace, and the genteelness of his acting.

There was little love lost between rival managers in those days of few theatres, but at least they gave each other the freedom of the house, which usually meant the freedom of the orchestra. Murphy relates that the eccentric John Rich of Covent Garden sat among the fiddlers at Old Drury on the night in February 1747 when Hoadley's long-popular comedy *The Suspicious Husband* had its happy send-off. For the play Garrick had written a witty epilogue embodying an ingenious fable:

> An ass there was, our author bids me say,
> Who needs must write; he did, and wrote a play.
> The parts were cast to various beasts and fowl;
> The stage a barn, the manager an owl.
> The house was cramm'd at six, with friends and foes,
> Rakes, wits and critics, citizens and beaux.

When Mrs Pritchard delivered the line " The stage a barn, the manager an owl," Rich turned to a friend seated by him and whispered, " He means me."

The privilege of the orchestra must have been peculiarly grateful to at least two of Garrick's friends—to Dr Johnson, because he was short-sighted, and to Reynolds, because he was deaf. Restricted, no doubt, as was the custom in the beginning, it cannot have been long established before a good many ordinary playgoers who noticed the presence of outsiders among the musicians and could either not see or hear well longed to occupy a similar coign of vantage. Good money—perhaps box price—

came to be offered for seats in the orchestra, and the players yielded to the temptation. It was not until the close of the eighteenth century, when, with the enlargement of the theatres, the orchestra well was extended from side to side, along the full width of the stage, that accommodation there became ample, and the increase in the custom seriously incommoded the musicians, and began to be looked upon as a nuisance. But it is much easier to establish a custom than it is to abolish it, and experience shows that when the attempt is made no half-hearted measures will suffice. Not to grasp the nettle is to be stung. On March 4, 1738, when Dalton's version of *Comus* was produced at Drury Lane, the bill presented the following intimation:

N.B. To prevent any interruption in the Musick, Dancing, Machinery, or other Parts of the Performance, 'tis hoped no Gentleman will take it ill, that he cannot be admitted behind the Scenes or into the Orchestra.

But nothing short of complete abrogation could have brought about any material abatement of the evil, and as long as the manager's friends were allowed to haunt the orchestra it was little use telling the public that seats could not be procured there. Their eyes told them otherwise. From time to time the old warning recurred in the bills, but the evil went on. At Drury Lane in November 1755, and again in February 1759, playgoers were fruitlessly informed that " No persons can possibly be admitted behind the scenes or into the orchestra." At a little later period one actually finds passes being issued on special occasions to the orchestra. In the Theatrical Museum forming part of the Widener Memorial Library at Harvard University there is preserved in the third volume of a Grangerized copy of Murphy's *Life of David Garrick* an undated order written by Garrick himself and reading:

> Mr Johnston,
>   Admit ye Bearer into the Orchestra.
> D. Garrick
>
> *Thursday*
> *24, for the Fund*

The fund here referred to was the Drury Lane Fund for Decayed Players, established by Garrick in 1766, and on whose behalf he was accustomed to give an annual benefit at which he himself invariably acted. Generously enough —especially for a man who was reputed to be stingy—he gave the entire receipts of his farewell performance to this fund. It still exists, but unfortunately is hampered by certain obsolete rules which nullify its usefulness. The pass was evidently given opposite a decent subscription to the fund.

Even in his later day Garrick himself was often to be seen seated among the musicians.[1] Together with Reynolds, he occupied a place in the orchestra at the *première* of Jephson's tragedy of *Braganza* in February 1775, and, in despite of his consummate knowledge of all the tricks of the trade, was so overcome by the pathos of Mrs Yates's acting as the heroine as to become visibly affected. Tears were to be seen trickling down his face.

Writing in her *Memoirs* of her *début* on the stage in

---

[1] "An Ode to Garrick upon the Talk of the Town," in *The London Magazine* for June 1749, written apropos of his recent marriage, begins with:

> "No, no; the left-hand box, in blue;
>   There! Don't you see her? *See her! Who?*
>   Nay, hang me if I tell.
> There's Garrick in the musick-box!
> Watch but his eyes; see there! *O, pox!*
>   *Your servant, ma'moiselle.*"

Which shows that the old term for the orchestra well lingered long.

the character of Juliet at Drury Lane on December 10, 1776, "Perdita" Robinson says:

> The theatre was crowded with fashionable spectators: the green room and orchestra (where Garrick sat during the night) were thronged with critics. . . . I shall never forget the sensation which rushed through my bosom when I first looked towards the pit. I beheld a gradual ascent of heads; all eyes were fixed on me; and the sensation they conveyed was awfully impressive; but the keen, the penetrating, eyes of Mr Garrick, darting their lustre from the centre of the orchestra, were, beyond all others, the objects most conspicuous.

So, too, when in after-years Mrs Siddons was wont to recall her succession of triumphs at Drury Lane in the epoch-marking season of 1782–83, memory always insisted on conjuring up a vivid mental picture of the divers notabilities who were then in the habit of sitting in the orchestra. "It was there," she once wrote, "that Sir Joshua always sat; and in that place were also to be seen— O glorious constellation!—Burke, Gibbon, Sheridan, Windham, and, though last not least, the illustrious Fox."

And so the practice went on and on. But the time came when it was deemed necessary to give the fiddlers a little elbow-room, and separate the sheep from the goats. When Drury Lane was rebuilt in 1812 benches were placed at either end of the orchestra well for the accommodation of the public. One does not know whether it was on one of these benches or actually among the fiddlers that Byron sat on the night when Edmund Kean played Othello for the first time before a London audience during his memorable engagement in 1814, but it is on record that the poet sat next to Michael Kelly, the composer, who was then musical director at the theatre, and that after Kean's thrilling outburst in the third act he turned to the genial Irishman and said, " Mr Kelly, depend upon it, this is a man of genius."

It is noteworthy that at Drury Lane at this period the actors belonging to the company were forbidden to sit on their off-nights in the auditorium proper, but were allowed to occupy seats in the orchestra. Can it have been that the lateral benches were established more or less for this purpose?

At Covent Garden on June 23, 1817, when John Kemble took his farewell of the stage in *Coriolanus*, such was the demand for seats that the orchestra was wholly occupied by spectators. Boaden, Kemble's biographer, was of the number, and recorded in after-years that, "being exactly below him," he " saw and enjoyed that amazing power by which an actor is enabled to subdue even his nerves to the temporary demand of the scene, and lay *himself* completely aside, to be resumed like a stage revival."

A little later the gentle Elia comes quaintly into the picture. This was at Old Drury on May 31, 1824, when Munden took his farewell benefit and appeared for the last time as Sir Robert Bramble in *The Poor Gentleman*. Having long been an admirer of his, Lamb was anxious to attend, but he had somewhat foolishly postponed applying for a seat in the boxes until it was too late, and he well knew that he was much too frail a being to attempt fighting his way into the pit on such a stirring occasion. Munden, having heard of Lamb's dilemma, and feeling that he had some return to make for the lavish praises showered upon him by the great essayist, went to the trouble of securing places for him and his sister in one of the corners of the orchestra. I leave Talfourd to tell the rest:

YOUNG JOE GRIMALDI'S DÉBUT INTO THE PIT AT
SADLER'S WELLS
From Cruikshank's plate in *The Memoirs of Joseph Grimaldi*, edited by Boz.

The play of *The Poor Gentleman*, in which Munden played Sir Robert Bramble, had concluded, and the audience were impatiently waiting for the farce, in which the great comedian was to delight them for the last time, when my attention was suddenly called to Lamb by Miss Kelly, who sat with my party far withdrawn into the obscurity of one of the upper boxes, but overlooking the radiant hollow which waved below us, to our friend. In his hand, directly beneath the line of stage lights, glistened a huge pewter pot, which he was draining, while the broad face of old Munden was seen thrust out from the door by which the musicians enter, watching the close of the draught, when he might receive and hide the portentous beaker from the gaze of admiring beholders. Some unknown benefactor had sent four pots of stout to keep up the veteran's heart during the last trial; and, not able to drink them all, he bethought him of Lamb, and, without considering the wonder which would be excited in the brilliant crowd who surrounded him, conveyed himself the cordial chalice to Lamb's lips.

From this time on the custom of sitting in the orchestra fell into desuetude, and was resorted to only on special occasions. When Maria Foote reappeared at Covent Garden on February 6, 1825, immediately after her action for breach of promise which had resulted in " Pea-green " Haynes being mulcted in £3000, excitement so far reigned in town that a vast crowd assembled at the doors of the theatre long before the hour of opening; and when at last they did open the rush was so terrific that within twenty minutes the house was full, and money began to be refused. Not wholly, however: box-frequenters clamouring for seats were coolly told that they were not to be had, but that the orchestra had been carefully fitted up for public accommodation, and that places could be had there at the modest price of two guineas. History does not record how many people submitted to this exaction, but its chronicles enable me to say that in this particular connexion it more than once repeated itself. When Charles Kemble's prolonged series of farewell performances began at Covent Garden in October 1836 the attendance was so consistently good that on November 21 the bill announced that on account of the great demands for seats " stalls had been fitted up in the orchestra," and places were obtainable there at 7s. each. The new seats were so well patronized that on the conclusion of Kemble's farewell nights in December the arrangement was maintained for the rest of the season.

When, in December 1873, John Hollingshead of the Gaiety sought to give a fillip to things theatrical in the dull nights before Christmas by putting up *The Hypocrite* and *John Bull*, with three stars in the casts—Phelps, Toole, and Charles Mathews—the booking in advance for the nine nights was so great that, rather than refuse good money, he displaced the band and converted the orchestra into stalls. In relating the circumstance in his *Gaiety Chronicles* he was evidently unaware that the thing had been done before.

The secondary use to which the orchestra well had been put throughout the eighteenth century and now and again in the century following evokes the question, To what part of the house does it legitimately belong? Is it part of the auditorium (as this old practice would imply) or of the stage (as might otherwise be inferred), or can it be that, properly considered, it is a separate section of the house? The problem bristles with difficulties, since it is puzzling to know on what principles the point can be determined. We have first to bear in mind that the orchestra well is a later accretion. It is a fundamental characteristic of the opera-house, not of the playhouse.

All that Shakespeare and Beaumont and Fletcher wrote had been acted before it came into existence. Its inception dates from the third decade of the seventeenth century, when the first public opera-houses were established in Venice; and, not being essential for drama, it was long before the principle became widespread.

Despite the obtrusions of the baton-wielding conductor, it cannot be maintained that the musicians form any part of the show. They are just as necessary as the prompter or the scene-shifter, but they are no more entitled to be seen. In the heat of action the normal spectator forgets their existence. It is nothing less than a misfortune that they should be visible. Wagner recognized this when he built the Bayreuth opera-house, and not a few managers of London drama houses have now and again hidden them from sight. The deduction, accordingly, to be made is that the orchestra well is a sort of No Man's Land.

On other grounds it can be argued that the well is not an integral part of the stage. In the age-long history of the theatre the highest, because most illusive, form of histrionic art has been attained under the rule of the law of the invisible fourth wall, and to nullify that law would be to enter upon an era of inferiority. It is true that in the lowest and most popular forms of theatrical entertainment the law has for some time been ruptured. In revue and pantomime direct communication with the audience is frequently indulged in, a foisting upon the theatre of the methods of the music-hall. But if the art of acting in the higher drama is to be maintained on the peak to which it has laboriously climbed the invisible fourth wall must continue to arise at the curtain-line.

It would be idle, however, to ignore the patent fact

that there is at present a strong tendency to return to the primitive, and to make the stage and auditorium one and indivisible. Convention is being flouted and novelty sought at any price. At one important theatre where Shakespearian representation is especially featured the orchestra well has been unnecessarily and unjustifiably pressed again and again into the service of the scene. In a revival of *Julius Cæsar* at the Old Vic in 1929, and in another later, the stage was connected with the orchestra by steps, and the mob ascended from the lower regions to the upper for all the world as if their normal habitat were the catacombs. It is symptomatic of the anarchy of the times that no one raised his voice in protest. Encouraged by the bland reception given to this cheap innovation, Mr Harcourt Williams, the producer at the theatre, went one better in the revival of *Macbeth* made in March 1930. After the knocking at the gate the drunken Porter descended into the orchestra to let in Macduff and Lennox, and later on the forces of old Siward scrambled up from the musicians' quarter on to the stage. The strange thing was that although there was neither rhyme nor reason in all this, it quickly met with silly imitation. When Tennyson's boyish effusion *The Devil and the Lady* was produced at the Arts Theatre on July 16, 1930, by Sir Nigel Playfair, the Satanic hero, instead of ascending from Hell through the orthodox trap, made his entrance from the orchestra well—not the most delicate of compliments to the fiddlers. It is all to the good that the playgoers of to-day should be open-minded, but ill-boding that they should have lost all sense of the fitness of things.

INDEX